*"For the kingdom of God
does not consist in talk but in power."*
1 Corinthians 4:20

POWER BEYOND WORDS

COMMUNICATION SYSTEMS OF THE SPIRIT
AND WAYS OF TEACHING RELIGION

by Allan Hart Jahsmann

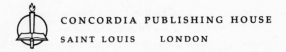

CONCORDIA PUBLISHING HOUSE

SAINT LOUIS   LONDON

Unless indicated otherwise, Bible quotations are from the Revised Standard Version, copyright 1946 and 1952 by the Division of Christian Education of the National Council of Churches and used by permission. Chapter notes appear in the back of the book.

The Leadership Training Committee and staff members of the Board of Parish Education of The Lutheran Church — Missouri Synod read the manuscript and gave many helpful comments. Particularly Dr. A. C. Mueller, Rev. Donald Hoeferkamp, and Rev. Delbert Schulz deserve far more than this inadequate word of thanks for their critique.

Concordia Publishing House, St. Louis, Missouri
Concordia Publishing House Ltd., London E. C. 1
© 1969 Concordia Publishing House
Library of Congress Catalog Card No. 73-76574

CONTENTS

FOREWORD

That there is always an urgent need for new life and spiritual renewal in the institutions of the church is hardly debatable. The need can plainly be seen in most local churches of the Western World, whether they are in suburbs, in urban centers, or still in the wildwoods. Though God, who is Life, cannot be dead, many parish churches are anemic and shriveled, or pompous but arthritic. All seem to be suffering — and some are dying — from the ravages of the times.

But the hope of the church does not lie in verbal barrages against "the times" or in defeatism. Nor is there hope in "business as usual," which is a type of defeatism. As it was in the beginning and ever shall be, the life-and-death struggle of any Christian church group can be won only by the resurrection and pentecostal power of God in its members and midst.

If this is true, and most Christians would acknowledge it to be so, then it is nothing less than tragic that the education programs and the *schools* of the parish often seem the *most neglected* and *sickly* part of parish life. For it is through the ministry of the Word of God (the proclaiming, communicating, and teaching of the Gospel) that the Spirit and kingdom of God still come in any time and place.

Even where there are dedicated pastors, professional ministers of education and youth, and Christian

7

lay leaders and teachers active in parish education, much that is done in the name of Christ and Christian education hardly seems imbued with the power of God and alive with His Spirit—and understandably so. It simply isn't true that a few people with a little love of Jesus (or still worse, a mere profession of such love) is all a church needs for an adequate and life-giving parish education program.

Even consecrated, well-meaning Christian leaders and teachers can be inept and ineffectual as teachers of the Christian faith and life. If we don't want to acknowledge our own shortcomings, we can think of others who have been poor teachers even though they loved God. Ability to teach is not necessarily in proportion to one's love of God.

The hope of the church is in its members who love God enough to become teachers of His Word in the ways by which *He* can get through them to others. So how can I become a better instrument or channel of God? This question could be put in many ways, and there is no single answer. But there are the best of reasons to ask the question and to look for answers.

There is real promise and hope in the current rethinking of religious education throughout the whole Christian church as a result of new insights in theology, education, and the psychological and social sciences. These findings, along with new modes of thought in the world today, offer new tongues and new vessels by which the church and churches can speak the Word of God to present-day children, youth, or adults *in the power of God's Spirit.*

God is eternal. The truths of His Spirit and Word do not change. But the world, which needs the Word and Spirit of God, is changing rapidly. And the

8

church's ways of communicating with the world can change and may need to. There have been many ways of teaching in the past, and there are many different theories of teaching today. Not all of them contradict one another simply because they are different. At the same time, not all ways of teaching are equally helpful for all times and purposes.

Since God must enter into the human spirit in order to give life, this book considers those systems of communication (call it teaching, if you will) that serve to communicate His Spirit and life to the human spirit. Though much more needs to be said about the subject, the book is offered in the hope that it may stimulate both clergy and lay members of Christ's church to reflect on their present parish programs and procedures. More than this, my prayer is that the readers will also honestly and seriously consider some of the alternative ways of teaching the Christian faith so that the church in their parish may flourish and not die.

ALLAN HART JAHSMANN

1

*In the beginning was the Word,
and the Word was with God,
and the Word was God.*

St. John

John 1:1

1

HOW GOD STILL SPEAKS

Many titles for this book came to mind: *Communicating God, Team Teaching with God, Teaching with the Power of the Spirit,* to mention a few. All of them seemed to permit the slippery notion that the communicator of the Christian faith (preacher, teacher, professing member, or parent) has a function separate from the actions of God.

Now, I believe what I've heard many Christians say: "Everything depends on God" — also in this matter of teaching others the Christian faith. To quote the Formula of Concord in its Solid Declaration (II 16): "Unless God Himself is our Teacher, we cannot study and learn anything pleasing to Him and beneficial to us and others."

But always the unanswered practical question was, How can I be a responsible servant of God, particularly in leading others into life with Him, and still be completely dependent on Him? Or to put the matter in reverse: How could I "leave it all to God" and still play a vital part in the process of communicating Him to others — or why bother to try if I am superfluous?

I recalled that some people have said: "You must get yourself out of the way in order for God to have His way in the lives of those you teach." But again there was the question, How can one get out of God's way and still be an instrument, a servant, a channel for God in His work? This, it seems to me, is a fundamental issue in Christian education.

I was prompted to search for some answers to the question by many experiences and observations of teaching that did not seem alive with the Spirit of God, even though what was being taught was "strictly kosher," "government approved," and straight out of the Bible. How is it possible that so much Bible preaching and teaching seems to bear little fruit? This can be a very disturbing question for anyone who seriously believes in the power of divinely inspired words.

Adding to the urgency of the problem is the challenge the church now faces in a dynamic but increasingly secularized world. This too is demanding a rethinking of the church's ministry of the Word and, in particular, its parish education programs and procedures.

At the same time and on a more positive side, a remarkably common interest in the dynamic forces of human relations and life has been developing in the psychological sciences, in philosophy, and particularly in the study of language and communication as such. Because these converging streams of thought are very relevant to God's business and the church's mission, it seemed important that church leaders and teachers at least consider the insights emerging from these studies.[1]

This book, then, is a study of various systems of communication by which God speaks or could teach through human agents, who are far from being divine. Though this text is only an introduction to the problem of how our human efforts in God's service can be the work of God, the hope is that it will lead the serious witness and teacher of Christ to some new and exciting possibilities. But first we must review the theology of the Spirit and the Word of God and the ways in which God speaks and reveals Himself.

The Christian View of God

With what images do you think of God? What do you "see" God to be? How do you envision Him? What are your ideas, your conceptions, of God? For instance, do you think of God mostly as a huge man with a long beard "up there" or "somewhere" in a place called heaven? This is the image we have inherited from Michelangelo and other artists of the Middle Ages. Is your picture of God usually that of a favorite portrait of Jesus? Or do you think of God by means of such signs and symbols as a triangle or an all-seeing human eye or perhaps as a dove or, less likely, as flames of fire?

Dr. Oliver Graebner of Valparaiso University once made a study of ideas of God.[2] He presented to children a series of pictures and asked them where God was in each picture. Where would you say God was in a picture of a fireman rescuing a person from a burning house or in a picture of a church-school class session? We say that God is present everywhere.

GOD IS A SPIRIT

The first basic truth about God that we shall have to repeat often to ourselves as we proceed to explore our problem was stated by our Lord when He said, "God is spirit" (John 4:24). God is *spirit*. That's the first point we must get. And a very important point it is—the starting point on which all right thinking about the workings and work of God is based.

The Bible speaks of God as Father, Son, and Holy

Spirit. But what do people understand and refer to by the term "Holy Ghost" or "the Spirit of God"? Just to answer, "God," is begging the question with a logical circle and gets us nowhere in a search for understanding. Nor will it help much to say that the Spirit is the Third Person of the Holy Trinity.

Far more significant are such questions as these: What *kind* of spirit is the Spirit of God? What does the Spirit *do* for Christians and through the church in the world? Can the life of this Spirit be communicated? If so, how? As we proceed in our study of the Holy Spirit in communication, we shall consider the nature of God in action rather than by definition.

But for the first let us simply admit (with some sense of need) that most Christians are still very fuzzy if not blank on what they mean by "the Holy Ghost." At the same time Christians are quite ready to accept the Bible's descriptions of God as light and truth and love and life, if not also as freedom and power. However, since God has been known as the Spirit of love and wisdom and light and life by people also in pre-Christian and non-Christian religions, let us briefly review what the distinctively *Christian* knowledge of God is.

GOD REVEALED IN JESUS CHRIST

"God was in Christ," wrote St. Paul (2 Cor. 5:19). "In Him the whole fullness of deity dwells bodily" (Col. 2:9). "No one has ever seen God; the only Son, who is in the bosom of the Father," wrote John in reference to Jesus, "He has made Him known" (John 1:18). "The truth is in Jesus," wrote the inspired apostle Paul (Eph. 4:21). Such has been the faith and witness of the Christian church in all ages.

Jesus revealed God as a loving, heavenly Father.

16

He taught His disciples to pray, "Our Father, who art in heaven" (Matt. 6:9), and He trusted, demonstrated, and taught the universal, fatherly love of God to the moment of His death. "My Father, if it be possible, let this cup [of suffering] pass from Me," He prayed in the Garden of Gethsemane. "Father, forgive them," He prayed on the cross.

Not only is *God* revealed by the life, death, and resurrection of Jesus Christ, but the way to *life* with God is revealed and made possible. "God was in Christ, reconciling the world to Himself" (2 Cor. 5:19). "I am the Way and the Truth and the Life; no one comes to the Father but by Me," said Jesus. (John 14:6)

So through Jesus, the Son of God as well as Son of Man, human beings can come to know and experience God as their loving Father, a Father who, like the father of the prodigal son, is always ready to forgive all His children their sins, accepting them by grace into the eternal kingdom of heaven in fellowship with Him. This is the good news Christians call the Gospel.

Incidentally we might already note, too, that this revealing, saving action of Jesus Christ is the identical action of the Spirit of God. Just before His death Jesus said to His closest disciples: "And I will pray the Father, and He will give you another Counselor, to be with you forever, even the Spirit of truth." And He added a little later: "The Counselor, the Holy Spirit, whom the Father will send in My name, He will teach you all things, and bring to your remembrance all that I have said to you" (John 14:16-17, 26). The Spirit proceeding from the Father and the Son keeps on talking inside the believers in Christ about what He said and did, and thereby reveals God and His way of salvation and life. (John 14:17)

The relationship between Jesus and God as Father is probably quite apparent to the reader (though never fully understood). But how can the truth that the Holy Spirit is God be related to the belief that the person Jesus is God and that God is His Father? This is more perplexing. Nevertheless it is equally necessary to see the latter relationships, for the Christian faith is that we can know God as Father only through the Son and that we can know the Son as God only through the Spirit of God.

Christian theologians have said that the whole matter is "above reason," meaning human reasoning. At the same time, however, they have attempted to formulate the relationships between God as Father, God as Son, and God as Holy Spirit. Their formulations are called the doctrine of the Trinity. Without denying the truth and value of this formulation, let us briefly note the confusion that may result from defining God as a trinity of persons while considering the Lord our God to be one Lord. (Deut. 6:4)

The God of the Bible is a triune God. As the Creed of Athanasius puts it, "Whosoever will be saved, before all things it is necessary that he hold the catholic [i. e., universal, Christian] faith. . . . And the catholic faith is this, that we worship one God in Trinity and Trinity in Unity." But this is a quite different conception of God than that suggested nowadays by the term "person" and by the statement that the triune God is three persons in one divine being.

Even when a distinction is made between three persons and one substance, the human perplexity is not eliminated, because God is like a person in His substance (that is, He is a personal God, a personal being). And it is difficult to think properly of the

18

Spirit of God as a separate person apart from God's incarnation in the person Jesus Christ. Many people who try end up with three Gods instead of one. They think of three persons existing separately alongside one another instead of within one another in what is called a unity of essence or nature.

So instead of explaining the triune nature of God as "three persons in one essence or substance," some theologians today are recommending that we might come to a very necessary understanding of God the holy Trinity by another way of thinking. They are suggesting that God might be more comprehensible in terms of a spirit. They maintain that we would "see" the triune nature of God by seeing the oneness of Christ's spirit with God as a loving Father and as the Holy Spirit.

At any rate, this way of thinking about God will be explored in the following chapter. For as we shall see, God reveals Himself as alive and a holy Trinity through the presence and Spirit of Jesus Christ. And *how* the triune God still comes and saves human beings, young or old, through Jesus Christ—that will be the main question.

But before considering more thoroughly how anyone can learn to know the triune God as the eternally loving, redeeming, saving God who is a spirit—the Spirit of life and grace and power—we must consider how this God reveals Himself.

The Word of Revelation

In the whole Christian church on earth today there is probably no subject more alive than the question, What is the *Word* of God? To put it another way: What is the Word that actually reveals God as He truly

19

thinks, feels, wills, and acts in His Spirit? To push the question still more toward our main concern: When and how does revelation take place as a spiritual *experience*, as an actual event, as a personal revelation in a present-day individual person's life?[3]

These questions can hardly be ignored, since we have already maintained that God is a spirit and that any revelation of God would therefore have to be a revelation of a spirit. The matter becomes crucial especially to those Christians who place great emphasis on the doctrine of the means of grace. This is the principle that God reveals and communicates Himself and enters into human life through His Word, never apart from His Word.

But also those who believe that *every* revelation of God is His Word of revelation must clearly define "the Word," because they need a norm for determining what is a revelation of God. To put it another way, we need a norm to "test the spirits to see whether they are of God" (1 John 4:1). Otherwise how could we escape the hellish possibilities that lie in interpreting personal desires or the promptings of the worst kinds of evil spirits as words of God?

What, then, is the Word, the seed of life in God's kingdom? (Luke 8:11)

REVELATION AND THE BIBLE

"The Bible" is the answer many, perhaps most, Christians would give when asked, "What is the Word of God?" In one sense this answer of course is true. Inspired by God, the prophets and apostles spoke and wrote *words* "taught by the Spirit" (1 Cor. 2:13; 1 Peter 1:11). "All Scripture is inspired by God" (2 Tim. 3:16) and therefore *is*, not only contains, the Word of God. By the words of Holy Scripture God *has* revealed Himself, His nature, His will, and most importantly His plan of salvation for mankind.

So when I read or hear or recall a passage, a sentence, or even just a word from the Scriptures, I can and may and in one sense do hear the divinely inspired Word of God. On the other hand, I may not. "Hearing, they do not hear, nor do they understand," said Jesus about people who did not get what He was talking about. In that sense they didn't get the Word and revelation of the Old Testament writings either.

We must also acknowledge that God has revealed Himself by means other than the Bible. "The heavens are telling the glory of God, and the firmament proclaims His handiwork. Day to day pours forth speech, and night to night declares knowledge" (Ps. 19:1-2). Furthermore, it's obvious that the God-revealing events, the "mighty acts of God," the "salvation history" reported in the Bible took place before the accounts were written and that all history, in a sense, reveals the hand of God.

Because the Bible communicates the revelation of God in the history behind the Bible, it is the revelation of God also in a historical sense. But at the same time we must recognize and acknowledge that much of the Bible is *not* revelation through history (God acting through human affairs). Many parts of the Bible present God in direct and verbal communication with people or give an interpretation of His actions or intentions: "God spoke."

Furthermore, the Scriptures are the revelation of God in an active, dynamic sense. We say they are "efficacious," that is, the Spirit of God reveals God through this Word. But before establishing further the role of the verbal word of the Scriptures in the communication systems of God and of His church, let

21

us note the need of the *Spirit* of God in the *communication* of the Bible.

Putting the concern bluntly, there can be misuses of the Bible that *fail* to communicate the Word of God or a revelation experience of God even though Bible words, verses, stories, or instructional sections and devotional songs are read, recited, referred to, or taught. In order to underscore this point, let us repeat it: The Bible can be misinterpreted or taught as something other than a revelation of God.

The Bible can be read and taught (even preached or performed) in such a manner that the words become *empty* of meaning and spirit. It can be presented as mere stories or moral instruction or as religious literature and history, and may not be received as an inspired *message*, a revelation of life and salvation. It can be drilled and grilled as words and facts for their own sake. It is often used legalistically in efforts to force people to accept a particular view of God, even though the view may be far from the whole truth or even false.

At this point we can already state as a self-evident but oft-forgotten principle that *the power of the Bible does not lie in the syllables, words, sentences, and stories as such.* The power is in God's Spirit. And it obviously isn't true that one can simply use words from the Bible, no matter how mechanically, and then—hocus-pocus, as if by magic—others will get God's Spirit and will grow in Christian understanding and faith. The words *as words* are *human* words and can be used without any kind of spirit.

The Word of the Spirit, the Word of divine truth, the Word of revelation, is in the inspired *content*

22

that the Bible words and instruction convey. The *meaning* and *message* of the truth lies in the spirit, and revelation is in and through the Spirit.

So we already have before us the very practical and important question of how one can guard against misperceptions and false uses of the Bible that lead to failures in the communication systems of God's Spirit. Another side of the matter is the question of how *others* are most likely to "get" (perceive and receive) a divine revelation through a use of the Bible.

THE WORD OF THE GOSPEL

Keeping in mind that the Word of God, properly speaking, is the inspired *content* and spiritual *substance* of the Scriptures and that the words are only the *form* and *vehicle* of the Word, we can readily see why the term "word" in the Bible usually refers to a message and way of life—the truth of life. The Bible calls the Word the Gospel, the word of the Kingdom, the word of the cross, the word of reconciliation, the word of salvation, the word of the Spirit, the word of Christ, the word of truth, the word of life. John called it "the truth of your life." (3 John 3)

This *Gospel* is the life-giving germ of the seed called the Word. The words are the shell. In this sense "Word of God" refers to the way of life that is in the heart and mind of God—in the Spirit of God. So God teaches, influences, changes, saves, and renews human beings through the inspired message of the Biblical words, not magically by the words as such. From this follows the practical principle that only when the Bible is received as Gospel (with what is called the Law of God in proper functioning relation) is the *Word* of the Scriptures communicated.

23

The truth of what we say about ourselves, in words or actions, is always in what we are. In the final analysis the truth about God is in God—in His reality, philosophers would say. God was incarnate and revealed Himself most fully and clearly as a person in the God-Man Jesus Christ. The Bible therefore calls Jesus the eternal Word who is God (John 1:1), the Power of God and the Wisdom of God (1 Cor. 1:24). He is the sum and substance of the Word that is called the Christian Gospel.

But still we must keep in mind that the word and revelation of the *Scriptures* is the source and norm of our present-day knowledge of God. Apart from the Bible record we can only speculate concerning the incarnate Word, the person Jesus Christ—what He said, what He did, the meaning of His life, death, and resurrection. Some present-day theologians have served us in refocusing our attention on the truly human man Jesus as the revelation of God, for He was and "is the image of the invisible God" (Col. 1:15). But it is by the *words* of Christ and of the Scriptures that we discover the meaning of His incarnation, His actions, His death and resurrection, and His teachings.

So nothing we must say later can detract from the essential need of the written Word of the Scriptures and the continuing need of human words in the revelation of the Spirit of God. But our point and principle of the moment is this: In order to receive the revelation of God in Jesus Christ it is necessary to study and communicate the Sacred Scriptures as *Gospel*—Gospel in the general sense of doctrine concerning Christ.

In this broad sense the whole Bible is the Word of Christ and the Word of the Holy Spirit, who is the Spirit of Christ and of God the Father. Martin Luther recognized that "all Scripture, when rightly viewed, has to do with Christ." He is "the Truth and the Life" and therefore the Word of divine revelation behind all Holy Scripture, the Alpha and Omega. "If you dwell within the revelation I have brought," said Jesus, " . . . you shall know the truth." (John 8:31-32 NEB)

FORMS OF THE WORD

The importance of the words of the Bible was indicated by the fact that God has spoken through these words and they are all related to the revelation of God in His Son Jesus Christ. "In many and various ways God spoke of old to our fathers by the prophets" (Heb. 1:1). But in themselves, apart from their use by God or people, words have no meaning—not even the words of the Bible. Their *meanings* depend on how they are used and what they refer to. The words in themselves are only forms and sounds that may or may not convey the Word.

The words of the Bible are perfectly human words in the original text as well as in any translation. When these words are properly understood and used to convey the truth of God in Jesus Christ, then they serve as a means by which God communicates His Spirit and a divine revelation—His Word —to human beings. On the other hand, when the words of Holy Scripture are used to convey some fact (historical or moral) unrelated to Christ and His way of life, then the words ordinarily *fail* to communicate the Spirit of God and a revelation of God.

A comedian on television once gave a satirical sermon on the fact that Esau was a hairy man, but

Jacob was a *smooth* man, according to the Biblical text (Gen. 27:11). He broke the passage into bits, explaining each word and phrase, and repeating the whole text often. But the message was a revelation of a ludicrous method of Bible study, not a revelation of God. I have seen the same method used in Bible classes—without the humor.

Let us also note the endless *variety of forms* in which the Word of God may appear. This point may seem obvious to some readers, but there are many people in the Christian church who limit the Word of God to words. Some even maintain, though never consistently, that only the verbal words of the *Bible* are the Word of God. People who hold this latter view usually allow for the words of the Bible in *other* words (translations from one language to another or in the same language), but in the past some have even limited their extension of the term "Word of God" to one or two particular versions.

It is quite evident that the Word of God is not limited *to* the words of the Bible, even though it is limited *by* the words when the Scriptures serve as the norm. The word of the Gospel can be proclaimed and taught in preaching, by the church's liturgy and sacraments, by theological and devotional writings, by church school Bible lesson materials, in private conversations, in group discussion, in hymns and other spiritual songs or poetry.

What isn't always admitted (or even permitted) is that the Word of revelation can also be communicated by means of a parable (fiction or an illustration from life); or by a play or a "sound" motion picture; or by any other use of verbal language, oral or written.

Even less likely to be acknowledged is the possibility that the voice of the living God can be expressed and communicated in a great variety of *nonverbal* languages. To mention a few: The Scriptures report that God often spoke to people through dream images. Who can say that He no longer does so? Freud and Jung uncovered the meaningfulness of all dreams. Furthermore, Christ and life in Him are made known by the very structure or forms of liturgy (the church year observances, the sacraments, the patterns and rituals of private and public worship).

Artists convey the Gospel and the Spirit of Christ through sculpture and architecture and picture windows and music and by all types of painting and illustration. Accompanying words often add clarity, but not always. Sometimes words limit and distract the viewer's thoughts.

Not to be ignored is the fact that God reveals and communicates His Spirit also when His people express His Word in human attitudes and actions. In this connection it's well to bear in mind, more than we usually do, that the Spirit of Christ lives in the living members of His body, since we say they receive the Spirit of God already in Holy Baptism. We also need to believe the words of Jesus that where two or three are gathered together in His name, there He is in the midst of them. (Matt. 18:20)

The apostle Paul pointed out that messages and meanings, the truths of the spirit, can be communicated most convincingly by human character and actions, both individual and corporate. He said that the expressions of Christian faith by the followers of Christ made them "a letter from Christ." What's more, this letter, "written not with ink, but with the Spirit of the living God, not on tablets of stone but on tablets of human hearts," was the credential of Paul's message. (2 Cor. 3:3)

27

The Word with Spirit

One last related point is introduced because it too will run through the remainder of the book. When understood, it becomes the capstone of all that has been said thus far. It is a further clarification of the organic relation between the Spirit and the Word and of *the necessity of receiving the Spirit through the Word* if a revelation of God is to be experienced.

It seems necessary to keep a distinction between Word and Spirit even though there is an inseparable relation between the two and we could properly identify one with the other.

It is possible to misinterpret and misuse the words of the Bible and assume (falsely) that the Word and thereby the Spirit are being communicated. One can talk, sing, read, preach, and teach about God and the Gospel without getting or giving the Word and thereby the *Spirit* of the words and Word. Just as a musician could play all the right notes and still not play the music with understanding and feeling—in the spirit of the piece—so we can also read or say all the right words and completely miss the interpretation and spirit of the words.

What is it that makes some words seem empty and dead while others (or at times the same words) come alive and have a power that touches and affects our lives? This is no trivial question. It is important to the whole mission and ministry of the church. The answers may give us clues to more powerful preaching and teaching of the Christian faith. Wouldn't that be something?

2

The Holy Spirit,
whom the Father will send in My name,
He will teach you all things.

Jesus

John 14:26

2

KNOWING PERSONALLY
AND BELIEVING IN

We have recalled in several ways that God is a spirit, that He is the Spirit of love and life, and that He is not three persons existing separately alongside one another but a "personal" spirit revealed as a loving fatherly person by the person Jesus Christ. We also noted that the Spirit of God is the Spirit of the person Jesus Christ and vice versa and that the Holy Spirit is the Spirit of God as Father.

Another principle that was established is that the *Spirit* of God is vital to the experience of divine revelation, regardless of the content and form of the communication. This applies also to the use of the Bible, whether we mean its words or just its content. The words and content must be "spiritually discerned," wrote Paul (1 Cor. 2:13-14), and that requires the Holy Spirit.

Obviously the question of "knowing God" is completely related to the nature of God, as will be the other subjects of this book. Facets of truth and spirit can never be tied up in neat separate packages. In this chapter we shall give further attention to the *experience* of revelation and the vital role of both the Word and the Spirit in this experience.

Who Really Knows God?

No one in a state of imperfection can know God fully. "Now we see in a mirror dimly. . . . Now I know in part," wrote St. Paul (1 Cor. 13:12). But when can I say, in a manner of speaking, that I truly (in the sense of really, not just rightly) know God?

Moses knew the Lord and even got to see Him a little, for "the Lord used to speak to Moses face to face, as a man speaks to his friend" (Ex. 33:11). Enoch walked with God, whatever that means. The early disciples knew Jesus personally even though they often didn't understand His words and actions. The apostle Paul said: "I know whom I have believed" (2 Tim. 1:12). What was the nature of their knowing?

As any philosopher will tell us, there are various kinds of knowledge or types of knowing. There is, for example, *factual* knowledge, truth in the sense of knowledge "about" some "thing" or person. When this kind of knowledge is more or less limited to observations and information and formal definitions, it is called "objective knowledge."

In contrast to a largely academic and scientific view that made a sacred cow out of *objective* data and knowledge, there is today in most fields of study a growing interest in what is called *subjective* and *personal* knowledge. This is a knowledge gained only by personal experience and insight, a knowing by faith, a knowledge of conviction.

We could consider this matter of knowledge and knowing in many other ways. We could, for example, approach the subject also through a study of how the *Bible* uses words for knowledge and truth. But we are primarily interested here in how one can get and give to others the knowledge of a spirit, particularly one that is "above and beyond" human reason. This is quite a different problem than that of merely gaining and giving information and an intellectual understanding of a subject.

We know the people with whom we live "better" than people we haven't met and have only heard about. In fact, we don't ever really know persons we haven't met, nor can we get to know them more than superficially unless they reveal themselves to us. For instance, you may have heard remarks about me, but you don't begin to know me the way my wife and children know me. And no one can really understand me unless I communicate with him.

Likewise no one can simply decide to know God and learn to know Him by "studying" Him as a subject or, rather, as an *object* of study. Nor can we hope to know God personally by a "purely intellectual" grasp of some statements and facts. "I believe that I cannot by my own reason or strength believe in Jesus Christ or come to Him," Lutherans say with Martin Luther. Nor can I teach someone else the Christian faith by *his* reason and *my* strength.

Because God is a spirit, a "personal" spirit (one who possesses in his nature the essence of what it means to be a person), He must be met and lived with in His Spirit before any human being can claim to know Him. When Job said, "I *know* that my Redeemer lives," he wasn't referring to something someone had told him; he was expressing a *personal conviction*. When the apostle Paul wrote, "I *know* whom I have believed," he was expressing a personal faith born out of personal *experience*. A genuine

33

personal faith is always the result of personal inner experience.

But how can God be experienced as He truly is in the reality of His being or existence? Another principle we can already state is: *Knowledge known as experienced revelation or gained by means of personal experience is, at least at some point, in the knower,* not simply in a book or in some other person. So, a personal knowledge of God must be something *within us.* This doesn't mean that the knowledge is entirely personal or subjective, without roots in the Scriptures and in objective truths of God. But it does mean that to know God personally we must meet Him in the life of our mind, heart, or spirit.

Today this learning to know God through personal experiences of His Spirit is often called "encounter." The word rightly suggests a personal communication experience in which the initiative remains with a second party, in this case God. God must come to man—from outside of man; we humans cannot simply "whip up" the experience. Those who try to do so deceive themselves and readily mistake their own thoughts and emotions for the Spirit of God.

But on the other hand, personal knowledge, in contrast to so-called intellectual knowledge and understanding, is *in the personal spirit and life of the individual person.* This means, then, that I can't know God until His Spirit is in my life and my life is His presence in me.

Furthermore, we already established the principle that to know the God of the Bible we must know Him not only as triune but also as a *person.* God is not an impersonal subject or spirit that we must study or search for in darkness in the hope that by searching we might find some glimmer of light and thereby get to know Him. "God was in Christ," says the Christian religion. In Jesus Christ God revealed Himself as a person who can be known in personal human terms. In fact, God revealed Himself as a person already in the Old Testament.[1] To know this God requires learning to know Him as we learn to know persons.[2]

THE KNOWLEDGE OF THE SPIRIT

At the same time we must remain aware of the fact that God is a *spirit*. It is seriously false and spiritually deadening to limit our ideas of Him to specific forms. By doing so we make idols. God can be truly known and experienced only as *spirit* — through knowing the Holy Spirit who is like wind and fire but who also has the nature of a person and lives in the hearts of God's people.

As it is written, "What no eye has seen nor ear heard nor the heart of man conceived, what God has prepared for those who love Him," God has revealed to us *through the Spirit*. For the Spirit searches everything, even the depths of God. For what person knows a man's thoughts except the spirit of the man which is in him? So also no one comprehends the thoughts of God except the Spirit of God.

Now, we have received not the spirit of the world but the Spirit which is from God, *that we might understand the gifts bestowed on us by God*. And we impart this in words not taught by human wisdom but taught by the Spirit, *interpreting spiritual truths to those who possess the Spirit*.

The unspiritual man does not receive the gifts of the Spirit of God, for they are folly to him, and he is not able to understand them because they are spiritually discerned. The spiritual man judges all things, but is

35

himself to be judged by no one. "For who has known the mind of the Lord so as to instruct Him?" But we have the mind of Christ. [1 Cor. 2:9-16]

So, God must be met and experienced as *spirit* in order to be truly known in the spiritual sense, and He must be met and experienced *in the Spirit and mind of Christ*. Because God is Love, He can be truly known only in the experience of the Spirit of love. Because God is Joy, He can truly be known only in the experience of joy. Because God is Peace, He can truly be known only in the experience of peace. The same can be said for all the other spiritual qualities of God.

In other words, there is a knowledge of God that only the experience of God's love can give, a knowledge that only the experience of God's joys can give, a knowledge that only the experience of Christian hope and forgiveness and care can give. By our very definition of this kind of knowledge we are saying that it is given *by* the experience of the *Spirit*. The *Spirit* communicates the knowledge. "When the Spirit of truth comes, He will guide you into all the truth," said Jesus. (John 16:13)

Knowing God as spirit and life also involves *living* in the Spirit, because the knowledge that the Spirit gives cannot be known apart from the effects of the Spirit on us and in our lives. In fact, this kind of knowledge gives the very life that the Word of life eternally promises. Jesus said: "I came that they may have *life* and have it abundantly" (John 10:10). Though the life Christ gives is eternal in the heavens, Jesus was talking first of all about human life on earth. Where else are repentance, faith, and godly living to take place?

But this life in the kingdom and Spirit of God,

36

we have said, is to be found in Jesus Christ and His way of life. The Christian Gospel maintains that *Christ* is the Way, *Christ* is the Word of truth, *Christ* is the Life (John 14:6). The eternal Spirit of God keeps on speaking the upward call of God in Christ in every age. So that we may "taste and see that the Lord is good," the person Jesus Christ must be loved and living in our spirit and life. Furthermore, our living in God depends on Christ living in us — individually and in the present. But this involves a certain type of faith.

A LIVING FAITH IN CHRIST

We could now consider different meanings of the word "faith," or what it means to believe, but to hasten on in our course of study, we shall immediately consider what *faith in a person* might be.

Faith in a person is primarily *a personal relation of trust.* We might think of a young child who has faith in his parents. Such faith becomes identical to the kind of knowledge we have been considering, the confident knowing that is gained through communing and living with a person in a relationship of love.

Knowing Jesus personally and believing in Him involve the experience of His Spirit and *trust* in Him. Such experience and faith are bound to lead to a love of God. "We love, because He first loved us" (1 John 4:19). It also creates a love of fellow human beings in actual human relations. "In Christ Jesus," said Paul, it is only "faith working through love" that counts (Gal. 5:6). "He who does not love does not know God, for God is Love," wrote St. John. (1 John 4:8)

As we all know (intellectually), the God revealed in and by Jesus Christ is the Spirit of love. We human beings have been the object of God's love especially in the life and death of His Son Jesus Christ. Through faith in Him we receive and accept the love of God. To the degree that we do not enter into the Spirit and life of His love (that is, "walk by the Spirit") in our personal lives with other people, we do not actually believe in Christ. "And this commandment we have from Him, that he who loves God should love his brother also" (1 John 4:21), for "if we love one another, God abides in us, and His love is perfected in us." (4:12)

So, in the process of knowing God *there is an indispensable relation between God's bestowal of love and our response.* But as we all know, even the best of Christians constantly fail to live their faith fully and perfectly. In fact, they often fall miserably into depths of sin. That is why those who try prayerfully to live the Christian life of love will say with the great apostle Paul: "I do not do the good I want, but the evil I do not want is what I do." (Rom. 7:19)

Such Christians can, however, say to themselves: "But one thing I do, forgetting what lies behind and straining forward to what lies ahead, I press on toward the goal for the prize of the upward call of God in Christ Jesus" (Phil. 3:13-14). And they renew their spiritual strength and mount up with wings like eagles by returning in repentance to God and drawing on His eternally forgiving love in Jesus Christ for the life of His Spirit.

The Word of the Living God

Continuing toward the main object of our study, we still have the question of how we can help others receive "the gifts of the Spirit of God" and thereby be "taught by the Spirit." The reader must patiently remember that we are only at the *beginning* of our pursuit. We haven't yet arrived at the practical answers. But we are on the way.

Before considering methods of receiving and communicating an alive and active Christian faith, a faith that expresses itself chiefly in actions of the Spirit of God within the human spirit, we need to look once more at the *means* (that is, the Word) by which the Spirit enlightens, calls, converts, and directs human beings. This time the question is, When (or how) do words and a word of meaning and truth become a *personally experienced* revelation of a spirit? More specifically: When (or how) does the *Word of God* become a revelation of the Spirit of God to me? It *is* a revelation, but when do I *see* it as a revelation in relation to my present and personal life and worlds?

THE BIBLE IN CONTINUING REVELATION

We are avoiding the expression "living Word," because the Word of God is always alive with the Spirit of God in an objective sense. On the other hand, the term "living Word" has been used by others with a variety of meanings. Sometimes the reference is to Jesus, sometimes to His church in general.[3] Occasionally it refers to the individual Christian's living or to a "live" communication. To avoid confusion and a debate about words, we shall be referring to "the Word of the Spirit" instead of to "the living Word."

Next we must acknowledge a historically well-established Biblical principle: Jesus Christ (and therefore also God as Father and as Holy Spirit) still speaks to us and will continue to speak to all human beings of any time and place *through the Bible*. This truth has to be repeated, because some theologians tend to forget the source and norm of the Word in their efforts to emphasize experience or Christ or the "living" aspects of the Word.

While the fundamentalists tend to worship the Bible and *words* (especially Bible words), and the high liturgical ritualists tend to worship other *forms* of the Word, the liberals are inclined to disregard Scripture and the traditional confessions of the church. They often belittle or deny the power of truth in verbal and propositional forms. "God did not reveal the statements of the Bible. He revealed Himself," says a recent, widely read book in theology.[4] But such statements make the very separation between Word and Spirit that modern theologians decry.

Partly because of theologians who speak of a continuing revelation of God *apart from* the revelation of the Scriptures, some people even within the church are asking: "Just what can I believe, and believe *in*, these days?" The searcher for God's truth and life need not be perplexed and "tossed to and fro and carried about with every wind of doctrine." The Gospel message that God was in Christ, loving and reconciling and saving mankind, "standeth sure." And in the Bible, which presents this Gospel, we have this eternal Word of God.

The Bible continues to be a present revelation of God also in another sense. "In many and various ways God spoke of old to our fathers by the prophets; but in these last days He has spoken to us *by a Son*, whom He appointed the heir of all things, through whom also He created the world. He reflects the glory of God and bears the very stamp of His nature, upholding the universe by His word of power." (Heb. 1:1-3)

So we are back to knowing God by knowing Jesus

40

Christ. But this involves knowing and understanding Christ's life, His suffering and death, His resurrection and glorious ascension. Knowing Christ and His teachings requires a knowing of the Old and New Testaments, at least to some extent. The foundation of the apostles and prophets, with Jesus Christ as the chief cornerstone that gives all of Scripture its proper direction and shape, is the basis of all Christian communication and faith.

THE NEED OF CONTEMPORARY INTERPRETATION

But though the canon of God's revelation of Himself has been closed, God continues to live as the everlasting Father, the risen Son, and the Holy Spirit *also in the present.* God reveals Himself—His nature, glory, and power—by the Spirit of Christ and the witness of His church—also in the world *today.* In Luke 24:48 Jesus related the witness of the Christian to the testimony of Scripture. "You [you, too] are witnesses of these things," and not just in the words of the Scriptures but also in your own words and deeds when they are prompted by God's Spirit.

The doctrine that the Bible contains all we need to know for our life and salvation certainly cannot mean that the Bible contains ready-made answers to all the questions of faith and life today and in the future. Nor can the Christian assume that he need not engage in prayerful and thoughtful study of the Scriptures for their present implications and applications. The live issue before us still is, How must I (or those with whom I communicate) *interpret* the Word of the Scriptures and of Christ in order for it to be recognized and received as a *contemporary* Word of the living Spirit of God?

Revelation is not only Biblical events and general

truths but also a present, personal communion between God and His people. The God who is an alive spirit always has revealed Himself in the real life history of human beings. Only when Christ appears as the ever-living, *present* Lord and Savior of the world in which we live—our personal Savior in the actual circumstances of our lives—is He taken seriously. The past apart from the present always seems irrelevant, and people who do not see God in their own present lives do not see God.

So, when does the Word take on significance *for me and my present as well as my future life and world?* The question is raised because the Bible was specifically addressed to the Hebrew people of Old Testament times or to Christian groups and individuals who lived in the Greek and Roman world shortly after the time of Christ. It was *not* addressed *directly* to us. And no one's life is transformed or saved merely by learning some Biblical facts and stories about people in ancient times or some instructions to *them* in the Bible.

To know Christ by His Spirit in our personal existence, we must relate the Scriptures as the Word of Christ to ourselves, our actual living and our contemporary life. To come to a present-day understanding of God and the life of His Spirit through the word of the Scriptures, we must somehow *translate* whatever was said specifically to Abraham or Moses or the ancient people of Israel, and to the people living at the time of Christ.

In other words, most of the Bible must not only be interpreted but must also be translated into *present-day* terms, both personal and social. One can't simply assume that whatever the voice of God told Moses is true for us and that whatever Paul wrote to the

Corinthian Christians applies to people today. Some ridiculous and even terrible mistakes can be made by such a false assumption. For example, try to apply the Levitical laws to yourself; or Paul's remarks about long hair and the wearing of veils. (1 Corinthians 11)

In wrestling with the necessity of making a jump from past revelations of God to present personal meanings and spiritual insights, some Christian educators have maintained that the Biblical accounts of past events and revelations speak for themselves. In one sense, of course, they do. So there always is the possibility that the mere presentation of Biblical material without *any* interpretation will produce in the hearer his own personal interpretations.

However, many people find that a bare presentation or reading of a Biblical event usually does not by itself communicate a present-day meaning. Often the inspired words of the Sacred Scriptures communicate to people false ideas or no meaning whatever.

MORE THAN BARE WORDS

Most of us probably would agree that to get a personal and present-day understanding of the Bible, children and youth as well as adults usually need something more than the bare recorded words of the Scriptures. Practically no one would consistently maintain that the best hope of getting to know God and of communicating His Spirit to others lies in limiting Christian education to Bible words, even though every now and then some well-meaning Christian demands such a limitation.

What we are trying to say — with great care because of the likelihood of misunderstandings — is this: In the past the living God revealed Himself to people in their historical and social contexts and never in a vacuum. The Bible is not simply universal pronouncements from on high, applicable in any time and circumstance without thoughtful (Spirit-directed) interpretation. Though God's revelation of His way to life and salvation in Christ is complete in our Sacred Scriptures, a living faith in the God and Father of our Lord Jesus Christ is related as much to the changing present as to the past.

To see the point in still another way: The communication of the Word of God in any form (whether it be through Bible reading, preaching, teaching, liturgical and devotional practices, witnessing, or visual and dramatic media) can be empty of spirit. It can be just words, hollow traditions, dead forms.

Communications that merely parrot or peddle "proper" statements — even if they are Biblical — are likely to be meaningless *to the hearer* though they be inspired and vitally important subject matter. As long as a message remains meaningless *to the hearer*, it is not a living Word and a revelation of the Spirit in the dynamic sense of a present, personal happening.

GOD SEEN IN THE PRESENT

What then seems to be required for a knowledge or faith that sees God alive and powerful in the present as He was in the past and ever shall be? How is His life-giving Word in the Bible and in the past experiences and confessions of His people most likely to "come alive" and be a living, vital, transforming Word of divine revelation for people today?

To be heard and received as the life-giving message of Gospel truth that it is, the communicated Word must be interpreted in terms of the needs, human relations, and actions of people living in the present. The Word must be heard and seen in present-day, concrete terms, especially those of the learner. If the communicator does not make any contemporary interpretations, the hearer and learner must do so for himself. Otherwise the learning that is defined in the next two chapters will not take place.

Most teachers of religion will agree that the application of a lesson is as important as the facts, if not more so. But Bible teaching that follows the formal steps of presentation, explanation, and application can easily become a largely factual study, with only a brief application tacked on at the end of the lesson.

Good teaching has been done with any method, but when we use the formal procedure established by the German educator Herbart, most of the activity is by the teacher instead of the learner. More often than not the applications are those of the lesson writer or the instructor rather than of the learner.

An extreme illustration of this would be a 30-minute description of the Old Testament tabernacle and its furnishings, followed by the concluding remark: "So here we see how we are to build churches and worship God." Such teaching is didactic, legalistic, and moralistic preaching imposed on the learner. Its weakness and failure lie in the lack of an experience of God's Spirit and the fact that the instruction is seldom taken seriously by the student.

For God to speak and be heard as a spirit, far more than a formulated application by the communicator may be needed. Furthermore, *the alive Word of divine revelation in its contemporary meaning is much more than an application tacked on to a general or historical Bible lesson.* To speak most directly to the spirit and life of the learner, the Word must be communicated as a present, personal truth of life.

Whether or not the Biblical Word of truth in its

life implications is more likely to be seen and heard in a movement from human life to the text or from a text to faith and life may be an unnecessary question. In other words, a great debate over the so-called inductive method versus a deductive procedure seems beside the point. The important issue is the need to associate the present with the past and to translate the past into present meanings, forms, and terms.

THE PLACE OF GOD'S APPEARING

One other point: To truly know God we must learn to know Him in our heart or spirit. But by heart we mean more than emotions or feelings, though the latter are involved. So is the mind. One can't "have a heart" without thinking. Having God in the heart is having a personal awareness and love of God as a result of seeing the light of the truths of God's revelations in Christ. Here again is the essential relation between Word and Spirit.

We might note further that faith alive in the human heart transforms not only one's view of God and relationship to Him but also one's entire view of the *world* and human *social* relations. "'Behold, I make all things new,' [said] He who sat upon the throne" (Rev. 21:5). And the apostle Paul exclaimed: "If anyone is in Christ, he is a new creation; the old has passed away, behold, the new has come." (2 Cor. 5:17)

Therefore, no aspect of present-day life can be excluded from the influence of God's Spirit without the individual and the world suffering some measure of spiritual death. The Spirit of God seats us "in the heavenly places" in Christ Jesus (Eph. 1:3). There we truly see and know God as He really is. But the Promised Land of heaven is not only on the other side of the river of *physical* death; it is the other side (the opposite) of *spiritual* death also in the present world in the lives of Christ's followers.

Furthermore, a living Christian faith is related to people especially in their social settings. "And by this we may be sure that we know Him, if we keep His commandments" (1 John 2:3). "If we *love one another*, God abides in us and His love is perfected in us. By this we know that we abide in Him and He in us, because He has given us of His own Spirit." (4:12-13)

So, when God, who is the Love manifested by Christ, lives through us, when Christ expresses and reveals Himself through us, then we too become His living Word, "a letter from Christ . . . written not with ink but with the Spirit of the living God, not on tablets of stone but on tablets of human hearts" (2 Cor. 3:3). And God's evident and most meaningful speaking in our present life is heard when we live by the Spirit of Christ in whatever relations we have with other human beings.

Some Educational Glimmers

We could already draw some practical conclusions on the basis of our theological considerations up to this point. In fact, the hope is that the reader has done so, for many of the theological principles we have pinpointed are at the same time *educational* principles. They point to the ways in which we must proceed if we truly desire to use God's systems of communication in our efforts at communicating His Word and Spirit.

The Spirit of the resurrected and living Christ in those who know Him will prompt them to speak the language of God's Spirit wherever they are—in homes, in schools, in the world, or in organized church relations and activities. The nature of this language that God speaks (also in worship services and church school classes) will be explored in Chapter 4.

But it should be evident from the foregoing that the Word of the Spirit ought not to be confined to words, much less to specific *forms* of words. Biblical words (in any form) are a means of receiving the grace and truth of God revealed in Jesus Christ, but the texts of Holy Scripture find their full Gospel meaning in the social and personal situations and happenings of human life today.

Of course, the *complete* revelation of God and His Word will not occur until the final great Day of our Lord. So from another viewpoint the Word of the Spirit must also be taught and received as a word of the future, a word of hope and of promise. Only with this note of promise does the Word remain *Gospel* in its spirit. This is why there is today a fresh and growing interest in "the Last Things" related to Christ's second coming.

But for now, let us begin to reflect on how we and our parish programs and life, particularly our church schools and our teaching of the Christian faith, may have to change in order to be more suitable systems by which God will truly enter into human lives. Our purpose, of course, is that *He* may come more fully into our homes, our churches, our church school classes, and our world.

3

The Spirit Is the Truth.

St. John

1 John 5:7

All who are led by the Spirit of God
are sons of God.

St. Paul

Romans 8:14

3

GETTING TO KNOW GOD

We have very briefly considered various views of revelation. Divine revelation is communication originating with God, who is a spirit. From at least one viewpoint it is any happening by which this Spirit makes Himself known to human beings.

We noted too that for this entrance of God into the world and life of men, *faith* is essential. Without faith the Word of revelation cannot be seen and grasped. We also set down the principle that the Word of God must be *interpreted* under the guidance of the Spirit of God in order that it be related to Christ and to present and future life in Him. Only by such interpretation is the unity of the Word and the Spirit of God maintained.

Because we must receive God's Spirit in order to know God, and because He must come to us repeatedly (not just in Baptism or on a rare occasion), we now move on to the question of how God gets through to us, granting that He may also be *in* us. We have adopted the principle that the source and channel of God's Spirit is His Word and that the Word is a message, a revelation, and also a person, a way of life, and a spirit—not just words.

The next basic question is, How can we and our students grow in wisdom and in the kind of knowledge that is spiritual understanding? We shall first consider how we "get" the message, the revelation, particularly of words (and therefore also of the Bible). Since it is possible to understand a message intellectually without getting the *spirit* of it, the second part of this section will begin to explore the even more important question of how people get the *spirit* of a message.

Getting the Message

How does God get through to us? I could undoubtedly dispose of this question simply by repeating the truth that human beings learn to know God through hearing His Word. Such a statement correctly assumes that the primary source of the knowledge of God is the Bible. But such a formulated statement can be a cliche' and a half-truth if it is not thoroughly thought out and understood. It just isn't necessarily so that all who hear and learn the Bible get to know God. That depends on what is meant by "hear" and "learn" and "know."

At the same time, the "Word" in various meanings we have reviewed is the necessary *means* by which God speaks to us. This Word (contrary to some philosophers, theologians, artists, and communication specialists) is largely in the form of *words* for which the norm is the written Word and words of the Bible. And words can have power—as much as any other form of language, if not more so. This is why we shall first relate some principles of *verbal* language to learning.

LANGUAGES AND MEANINGS

Here we cannot enter into a lengthy discussion of what language is or how languages develop and change. Nor shall we consider the differing views as to when language expressions are meaningful. Although these subjects are relevant to our concern, for the moment let us note only a few points: (1) All expression and communication is language, and vice versa; (2) language is empty unless it communicates what it speaks; and (3) before we can discuss whether a statement or an interpretation of it is true or false, we must have some idea of what the statement means.

We also need to remember that language has its *primary* meaning in the specific situation in which it is used. The principle is this: *The meaning of language lies mainly in its use.* To understand what I say to you directly, you must know far more than the words and grammar. To see this, try translating with a dictionary a letter written in a language you don't speak. Words can mean different things at different times, have different levels of meaning, and often mean different things at the same time. One of the best examples is the word "love." You must get what I am referring to through the *way* I say it and through associations that are common to both of us.

All this has said nothing as yet about the *connotations* (the *personal* meanings) that people get from or can read into any expression or communication. Michael Polanyi maintains in his book *Personal Knowledge* that there is a personal element in all knowing.[1] Many psychological studies in recent years have indicated how the message people receive differs from person to person even when the objective message remains exactly the same.[2]

The various factors that can play a part in our personal perceptions and understandings of a subject is another interesting study. But let us move on to a few principles that may help us uncover *literary* meanings even when they have been expressed in the distant past, for we are first of all concerned with the messages of the Bible. These, as we all know, have been communicated to us through words and sentences, that is, human writing.

Here we must briefly touch on the science of hermeneutics, the principles that help us translate, explain, or interpret any piece of writing correctly. A compact, fresh, and readable summary of these principles for interpreting the Sacred Scriptures is Herbert Mayer's *Interpreting the Holy Scriptures*.[3] For our purpose let us focus on the fact that the meaning of any statement is to be found (and therefore sought) mainly in the way it was and is used.

In other words, the sense and significance of a passage depend not so much on letters, syllables, words, and combinations of words but on that which is communicated by means of the words *in the way they function*. Because the meanings of the words and expressions of speech are established by the experiences of ordinary human life, the living human context is far more important than words as such, or grammar and syntax, or even the verbal context.

Of course the words are important too, especially in establishing preciseness of *factual* truth. Hebrew and Greek word study and grammar have played a basic role in the interpretation of the Bible. But the science of semantics (from the Greek word *semantikos*, meaning "significance" or "meaning") has indicated that the traditional emphasis on word studies and cross-references can be very misleading.[4] The truth of a literary document may more readily be found through other avenues of approach, and so may the truths of Christ that the words of Scripture convey objectively by God's intent, but often not subjectively, for various reasons.

What are some other approaches to a literary document, such as the Sacred Scriptures also are? How can we get at the meaning of a book as a whole or the meaning of a given event or statement? More specifically, how can one uncover and discover Jesus Christ and His word of the Gospel in the *forms* of the word of Scripture? The problem is evident especially in relation to those sections of the Bible that seem to have no reference at all to Christ and faith in His way of life.

In his book on interpretation Professor Mayer discusses four circles of context that he says a Bible student must consider: (1) the sections preceding or following a given word or passage, (2) the entire book or letter in which the passage appears, (3) *all* the writings of a given author in order to discover his pattern of thought and style of writing, and (4) the entire Bible—its nature as Gospel and salvation history, its purpose, the chief themes, etc.

To these considerations and the context of history and culture (which Professor Mayer also mentions), the science of semantics is adding its accent on the *sender* of a communication (his thoughts, feelings, and actions) and on the *receiver* (his relationships to the sender and his attitudes, perceptions, and responses). Also the Bible student and teacher must keep in mind that words have only the meanings that persons, divine or human, give to them in a human situation and in a specific live communication. The objective message and meaning is what the *sender* refers to in the communication or text. The subjective meaning is what the *receiver* gets as the message or word. In the case of the Bible, we get its objective truth subjectively only when we get the *Spirit* of its messages and message. "The Spirit," said John, "is the Truth." (1 John 5:7)

Many students and teachers of the Bible get lost and bogged down in the *words* of Scripture, which are *not* addressed directly to them. In a very positive sense we can say that the Bible refers to problems, situations, and events that are ancient history. This history becomes relevant and meaningful to people in the present only as its truths are somehow translated into their personal and social lives.

Because the *Spirit* is the Truth and the truth is in the ever-alive, ever-new *Spirit* of God, we must look for the *contemporary* meanings in the story of God's dealings with the people of Israel and in the New Testament story of Jesus and His love. Before we consider direct ways of understanding the present-day meanings of the inspired texts of the Bible, we must also acknowledge, at least with a passing glance, the nature of religious language and particularly the language of the Bible.

RELIGIOUS LANGUAGE

In recent years many studies of religious language, God-talk, and the language of the Bible have been published. Here are only a few conclusions of the scholars:

The books of the Bible, though written by men who were inspired and moved by the Holy Spirit, were written in the language of their authors. The original texts were also in the *Rede*, the living speech, of the people to whom they were addressed.

These languages, like all words and expressions, did not get their precise meanings from a code or dictionary of definitions handed down by God on golden tablets. Their meanings, in general, emerged in the life experience of both the writers and the original receivers. In other words, the languages of the Bible were the ordinary speech of both the senders and the receivers and served as a common medium and vehicle of communication.

We don't always work with the fact that God speaks most clearly in the language of the people He addresses — or we don't want to believe it (for various reasons). For example, many Protestant Christians still believe that the King James English is more "religious" than present-day kinds of pop-talk, and "high" churchmen feel that Latin words are particularly appropriate for references to God and communication with Him. Table prayers at Oxford University colleges continue to be said in Latin even though very few students understand them.

In any case, we need to know that language which talks effectively about God has some distinctive characteristics, according to studies of religious language. For example, Ian T. Ramsey maintains that revelation (he calls it moments of "disclosure" in which "the light dawns" and the "ice breaks") seems to be experienced most often through language that is "odd." This language, he says, is more like poetry than prose, more often symbolical and para-doxical than logical. Take, for instance, almost any sayings of Jesus in His Sermon on the Mount. Other writers have called it "meaningful nonsense." This kind of language seldom is found in statements of propositions and definitions.

Some people distinguish between language that communicates facts and language that expresses and touches human feelings or emotions. The latter

57

sometimes disparagingly is called "emotive" language or propaganda. But the language that turns on the light of eternal truths and actually stirs the *imagination* of the human heart is quite different from emotional propaganda or sentimental and even eloquent language. It differs also from language that communicates facts and truths as straightforward information.

Powerful language that opens up and illuminates faith and life is largely symbolic; that is, it does not *directly* disclose what is symbolized and communicated; it communicates its message *indirectly, only partially, and through personal connotations as well as through objective truth.* The scrawled statement "I quit school when I were sixteen" on a New York billboard said much more than the fact that the writer quit school at age sixteen. Students of religious language have noted that all religions make much use of indirect kinds of language, such as similes, metaphors, analogies, parables, myths, etc.

Another related and interesting point: Truly religious language does not limit itself to observable facts, nor does it tell all "in plain English" that no one can miss or misunderstand. God-talk that reveals spiritual truths is never impersonal and mere information. It is what some writers call "passionate" language. This kind of language is what Donald Evans calls the language of self-involvement, language that utters something that really matters to the communicator and calls for a decision and a commitment.[5] This is the kind of language found in the Bible.

Passionate language, though full of feeling and concern, is nonetheless factually precise and true. But the precision is the precision of passion. In the Scriptures it is the passion of God's heart of love for the world and all its inhabitants. Said Martin Franzmann in *Interaction:*

> The precision of passion is obviously different from the precision of thought. (Although theologians are always tempted to forget this and to make bad alliances with philosophy, the worshiping church knows better and allies herself with poetry. This is why old hymns stay fresh long after old theologies have gone stale.) The inspired chroniclers of the mighty acts of God are not "good" historians according to our prim secular standards; they are amazingly free in their impassioned recitals. They omit all manner of important matters, like the first 30 years of the life of our Lord or His physical characteristics. They condense and expand with a nonchalance that drives sober historians mad. Who can write a "real" *Life of Jesus* or a *History of the Early Church* on the basis of the materials which they provide? But they do manage to say, "Come unto Me!" and they say it very powerfully.
>
> Above all, these men who, impelled by the Spirit, speak from God and for God knew that there is no . . . more "factually precise" way of saying "The Lord is my Shepherd" than to say, "The Lord is my Shepherd." Paul wrote with passionate precision when he spoke of the tribunal and the judge, of fathers and sons, of the body and its members, of the footsteps of Abraham, of love poured out in men's hearts, . . . of being sold under sin, . . . of engrafted branches, of leaven, of building up people, of crowns, . . . thieves in the night, ransom, the lion's mouth, the trumpet, gongs and cymbals, . . . and much more besides. And who can recall the Jesus of the Fourth Gospel without thinking in the images of the Lamb, the Temple, the Bridegroom, the Bread of Life, the Light of the World, the Door, the Shepherd, the Way, the Vine? [6]

Getting the Spirit

What then are ways to a *spiritual* understanding of God, ways that will help us know God in His *Spirit*, ways that will enable us to speak for Him by His Spirit speaking through us? Let us pursue the foregoing in search of some further principles that may point us to God's illumination of the human mind and heart.

WAYS TO UNDERSTANDING GOD

Perhaps we should first review ways of knowing and understanding so that what we previously considered will help us in what we hope now to see.

There is a difference between what the Germans call *Bedeutung* and what they mean by *Sinn.* The first word refers to what something denotes; the second refers to its significance and more personal meanings. A person can know a lot of words, facts, and formulations in one sense and understand none of them. Pestalozzi said of some children: *"Sie kennen viel und wissen nichts"* ("They are acquainted with much and know nothing").

Though individual words and facts are sometimes very important, they are often relatively unimportant in themselves, especially when compared with the knowledge that the Bible calls wisdom or understanding. Insight into the personal meanings that a religious communication might have for me is essential to my understanding of God as the Spirit alive in my life.

Without some understanding of present personal and concrete social meanings, my faith remains in the head, and dead. The development of this kind of insight is therefore of paramount importance and ordinarily requires something more than a brief "application" by the communicator at the end of his message or lesson.

So, what fosters and facilitates the understanding of *present meanings* of the Gospel? What serves to bring about *insight or discernment*, "truth in the inward being" where God wants it (Ps. 51:6), the kind of understanding that grows *within* a person? That's still our main question.

In looking briefly at religious language and the language of faith, we noted that the dynamic, God-inspired language of the Bible is full of imagery expressed in symbolic words, expressions, and stories. Ezekiel spoke of dry bones and wheels, and Jesus pointed to sheep and fig trees in talking about people. This kind of language calls for *thinking* and *comprehension* in order to be understood and truly known.

The Bible is not a book that simply requires the teaching of facts and mere memorization and recitation. It reports that when Jesus taught, He spoke in riddles and figurative speech so that hearing what He said, people would not immediately "get" what He was talking about but would have to *think.* (Matt. 13:34-35)

We mentioned the paradoxical nature of religious language. Such paradoxes are contradictory nonsense when taken literally, but when considered thoughtfully and in Christian faith, they are true and deeply meaningful. For example, Jesus said: "I have not come to bring peace, but a sword" (Matt. 10:34), even though He also told His disciples, "Peace I leave with you" (John 14:27). Paradoxes require thinking. Their sense is not obvious without reflection.

When we accept something without thinking it

61

through for ourselves, we don't get the whole truth —we often get only a half-truth or surface facts. Nor do we make the object or truth of faith a part of ourselves, a vital part of our own being and living. Jesus required His disciples to think about His subjects as a means of leading them to see spiritual truths for themselves.

But still the question: What helps me see *present* meanings of past events and revelations, particularly those in the Sacred Scriptures? What we teachers of religion have been calling "the application" is often only a parting conclusion or summary of the point or lesson. The real application may be in the whole communication process. Let us at least consider this possibility.

Psychological studies of the process involved in getting insight indicate that the bridge from words to meaning, from a Word of the past to the grasping of its message for the present, usually involves a degree of personal concern, some conflict or doubt, some wrestling of a person's spirit with the angel of God. These findings suggest that surprise, contradiction, puzzling ambiguity, the challenging and testing of that which people take for granted may be keys to the kind of learning we are exploring. We all know that platitudes and boring repetition of the familiar are among the worst enemies of the spirit —God's or our own.

Curiosity leads us to get our own understanding of a subject, and that holds true also for religion. But how many Christians are genuinely curious about the life of their spirit? How many people want to learn more about God, the teachings of the Bible, and the Christian faith and life? The answer can be seen in most parishes, even in their church schools.

But a more hopeful answer, my friend, is blowing in the wind, as a folksong suggests.

What other factors are involved when we experience a glimmer of insight and get what Martin Buber called "the shudder of self-identification" through a communication even when it does not speak about me or to me directly, as in a play or other types of art? Certainly our experiences and our own associations play a part when something we see and hear "rings a bell" inside us and starts a train of thought. Let us therefore continue to explore the conditions usually present when people receive the illumination and light of God's Spirit.

OTHER CONDITIONS OF ILLUMINATION

All spiritual illumination comes through some kind of communication. Another principle we can accept is that *conscious spiritual awakening and comprehension within a person ordinarily occur only through communications that are appropriate to the developmental level of the learner.* Even though we sometimes underestimate an individual's ability to understand and learn at a given age or stage, much teaching of religion is not comprehended and appropriated because it is not *appropriate* to the learner. The laws of human development apply also to religious experience and growth.[7]

In other words, a communication must be on the same wave length as that of the receiver. Furthermore, the receiver must be hooked up and turned on, and must be in tune with the message and spirit of the communication in order to receive it. If, for example, religious communication addressed to youth is completely foreign to their lives and gives answers to questions they have never asked or are tired of hearing, the chances of their receiving a revelatory experience are not very great, no matter how Biblical and orthodox the messages might be.

Even less promising is a teaching of religion to young children in abstract, intellectual terms, as is so often done. Consider, for example, the catechism definition of the two natures of Christ and how they "partake" of each other's attributes. Several large studies have concluded that before the age of 11 or 12 children are unable to understand abstract religious concepts and doctrines in the way adults formulate them.

On the other hand, young children are far more ready than adults to enter into the world of feelings and actions. They can sense a spirit of mystery, love, joy, tragedy; and they respond to it especially when a spirit is communicated by persons. This may be the reason for the remarkable statement of Jesus that "unless you turn and become like children, you will never enter the kingdom of heaven" (Matt. 18:3). So at least in teaching young children we ought to deal far more with feelings and actions than we usually do.

Also to be considered on any age level are the attitudes and values of the learner, his background and viewpoints. They play a decisive part in what is heard, seen, and learned. This fact, too, points to the need of the Holy Spirit, a *right* spirit, *within the person receiving the Word.* It also reminds us that spiritual understanding seldom, if ever, comes to a person without periods of preparation and reflection. The "Aha!" of insight doesn't just happen in a vacuum. Like corn, said Jesus, the seed of the Word grows to fruition silently in the night.

The group stance, the spirit of the group, is another

distinct factor in the experiencing and gaining of God's Spirit. Even though there undoubtedly can be exceptions to the rule, most of us learned to know God through relationships with His church. And the quality of our faith and Christian life most certainly has been and will be determined by the extent and quality of our relations and life in our homes and churches.

An old saying is that a Christian without Christian relations is like a log that has rolled away from the fire. Even if it is burning a little, it is likely to go out soon. All of us know how difficult it is to remain Christian in a non-Christian group. The church is the living body of Christ. Where His Spirit is strong in its members, they relate to other members of the body and mutually build one another up in the Christian faith and life, even as St. Paul described the process in 1 Corinthians 12.

A particularly important aspect of this church fellowship for Christian faith and life is the teacher-learner interaction. The human, personal factor in religious communication has been greatly underrated. A communicator cannot speak a word he himself has not heard. Jesus once asked: "Can a blind man lead a blind man? Will they not both fall into a pit?" (Luke 6:39)

In addition to the knowledge the teacher shares, there is the even greater influence of the teacher as a person. Most of us can point to a specific individual or two who have influenced our lives much more by what they *were* to us than by what they *said* to us. Studies in psychotherapy have demonstrated that personal relations and identification models (individuals who are greatly admired) are major determinants of a person's character and behavior. They

65

are therefore a vital part of learning experiences designed to develop Christian character and behavior.

Of even greater importance to the learning of religion than to any other subject is the nature and quality of the setting and the set — the arrangements and the atmosphere of the learning situation. This will become evident in the discussion of the absolute need for a climate of freedom and love. For a relaxed, warm, and social feeling, small face-to-face groupings in pleasant informal surroundings are preferable to large formal assemblies.

A breakdown in communication can take place also in the *process* of communication — in the methods as well as by the language used. But further discussion of these important considerations must be delayed for the moment.

Taking the Word to Heart

While acknowledging the traditionally recognized need for information, I have emphasized that the meeting of God through His Word is in its *meaning* or spiritual *truth*. It is only in the service of truth that words and facts take on value.

Of course, the truth that sets us free and gives us the life of God's Spirit is not just *any* truth; Christians believe it is the Word of the Gospel incarnated in Jesus Christ. This truth is not in a dead Christ of long ago but in the resurrected Lord, who lives in His body, the church, and in the personal and social lives of its members.

Even Bible words, we must remember, can become empty words, nothing but talk, when they are used without their spirit, as the apostle Paul so eloquently taught us in 1 Corinthians 13. They can also be *heard* as mere words. This is why Jesus often warned people to "take heed" how they listened and heard.

On the other hand, words serving the Word of the Spirit are the power of God. When God speaks, something happens. "And God said . . . " and it was done. His Word conveys almighty, creative power.

His Word is also a saving power. "The Gospel . . . is the power of God for salvation to everyone who has faith" (Rom. 1:16). Today most students of language recognize that words can perform or bring into being the actions they express (as when someone in authority says, "I appoint you to be the chairman").

We also started to consider some ways in which the Word becomes luminous, is seen clearly and brightly, and then like a sharp sword pierces the very joints and marrow of a person's body and the thoughts and intentions of the heart (Heb. 4:12). All these preliminary considerations present us with some inescapable educational deductions. They point to the kind of process and programs that are needed if the Word of God is to be experienced in the power of the Spirit.

Getting to know God, "getting to know all about Him," requires communication with Him—through His Word but by His Spirit. The practical chapters on methods and media are coming. For now, you may find it interesting to write down what *you* can already see are some inevitable educational conclusions concerning the teaching of religion.

4

---

*O dry bones, hear the word of the Lord.
Thus says the Lord God to these bones:
Behold, I will cause breath to enter you,
and you shall live.*

Ezekiel

Ezekiel 37:4-5

THE LANGUAGE GOD SPEAKS

Lord, speak to me that I may speak
In living echoes of Thy tone.

So go the opening lines of a popular hymn by Frances
Havergal. Before we can speak for God, we must
learn to know Him as a spirit and in His Spirit. But
for us to know God as He exists in His Spirit, He must
somehow communicate with us.

How does God still speak to at least some human
beings in the world today? What would you say?
The question "What is the *Word* of God?" was considered in Chapter 2. Here we must assume agreement that God spoke both to the Old Testament
prophets and to the New Testament writers of our
Sacred Scriptures.

I shall also take for granted that God *continues* to
speak not only through his original revelatory actions
in times past but also through the inspired *record* of
some of these revelations, if anyone wishes to make
a distinction. Precisely because there is the necessity
of hearing God speak in the present through *past*
revelations of Himself, let us now consider the Word
of God in terms of His *Spirit.*

In a very basic sense, *every* communication and
revelation of God is His *Word.* "In the beginning
was the Word . . . and the Word was God" (John 1:1).
And there is an inseparable relation between the

71

Spirit and the Word, just as there is perfect identity between the Word of God and the person Jesus.

But we began with the principle that God is a spirit and they who worship (and teach) Him must worship (and teach) Him as a spirit. Perhaps we therefore need to consider what kind of spirit God is before we can agree on how He speaks in a spiritual sense.

The Spirit of the Lord

What kind of spirit is God? Thinking abstractly at this point, what could we say? Love? Freedom? Hope? Joy? Life? We probably don't often think of God in these terms, but why not? Of course much more could be said about God, but the point of most agreement on which we might move ahead together is that God is Love, the Spirit of pure love.

THE LOVE THAT IS GOD

What do we mean when we say with St. John that "God is Love" (1 John 4:8, 16)? The truth of this statement, like that of any other, depends on its meaning. There are at least "57 varieties" of love. There is puppy love and a love of life; a love of parents, children, friends. Most people "love" to eat and "simply love" certain kinds of food. There is the love of a man or boy for his dog, and the love that is simply selfish desire even between so-called lovers. In each case the word "love" has a distinctly different meaning.

But "in *this* the love of *God* was made manifest among us," wrote St. John in describing the nature of divine love, "that God sent His only Son into the world so that we might live through Him" (1 John 4:9). By faith we can see the love of God in all His creations

72

and actions. But above all, wrote the inspired apostle Paul, "God shows His love for us in that while we were yet sinners Christ died for us." (Rom. 5:8)

So according to the Scriptures, God's kind of love was revealed most gloriously in the death of Christ for the life of the human race. In His death and resurrection we Christians see the love of God most clearly. But this was only a manifestation of God's love, though the greatest manifestation. Can we say that God no longer speaks by His Spirit or that He speaks only through past events?

God's love is not only *revealed* in the self-surrender and death of Jesus Christ, "who loved us and gave Himself for us"; His love is also *poured into the hearts* of all who believe in Jesus Christ. "God's love has been poured into our hearts through the Holy Spirit which has been given to us," wrote St. Paul to the Christians in Rome (Rom. 5:5). From Jesus, the King of Love, the divine Fountain of Love, flows the living Spirit of the God who is Love, the Holy Spirit of *agape* (the Greek word for the kind of love God is).

From this God-Man Jesus human beings receive the Spirit of God and become capable of expressing God's kind of love. In fact, says St. John (as did Jesus), only as we express this love particularly in our interpersonal and social relations do we have the Spirit of God. "We know that we have passed out of death into life, because we love the brethren. He who does not love remains in death." (1 John 3:14)

So what are we saying? The Spirit of God is the Spirit of love incarnated in Jesus Christ and most vividly revealed by His self-sacrificing, redemptive life and death. That's the central theme of the Christian Gospel. Christ's love is also the determiner of life in the eternal kingdom of God, for His Spirit produces love (Gal. 5:5-6), "the love of the Spirit." (Rom. 15:30)

The Spirit of God is the source of a human love of God and a human love of people as well. In fact, properly understood, the two are identical: "If anyone says, 'I love God,' and hates his brother, he is a liar; for he who does not love his brother, whom he has seen, cannot love God, whom he has not seen" (1 John 4:20). "If we love one another, God abides in us, and His love is perfected in us," wrote the inspired-by-God John. (1 John 4:12)

So the hallmark of the living presence of God is love, and in a properly understood sense, God continues to love by *our* love. By our actually loving real-life people, said John repeatedly (see especially 2 John and 3 John), we not only walk or live in the truth; we also become supporters of the truth and workers in the truth (3 John 8). By our love, so to say, God speaks the truth of His Spirit. "So faith, hope, love abide, these three; but the greatest of these is love. Make love your aim," wrote Paul (1 Cor. 13:13 — 14:1). Without it we and the church and its message are nothing.

Perhaps, then, we ought to think of religion chiefly as the practice of love; and the teaching of religion as the teaching of love; and the communicating of the life of God's Spirit as the living out of the Spirit of love. Why not? When the church loves, she has God's power and attractive beauty.

All this does not imply that faith is unnecessary, for it is by faith that people receive Christ and His divine love into their lives and gain the power to become the sons and daughters of God. But the point here is that "all who are led by the Spirit of God are sons of God" (Rom. 8:14), and only those. "He who does good is of God; he who does evil has not seen God." (3 John 11)

Because love is truly "a many-splendored thing," we might test our understanding of it by seeing how we would complete the sentence, "Love is _____." Love is the act of forgiving and accepting. Love is showing concern and kindness. Love is valuing another person's existence. Love is giving of oneself to another person. What else could we say love is? Stop and think for a few moments.[1]

THE LANGUAGE OF LOVE

Instead of looking at love as just an abstract subject, let's bring the subject more closely into our lives by considering what it means to be loved and to love another human being.

In view of the fact that love is essential to human life, one might expect most people to have a great deal of understanding and concern about love. Especially might one expect to find a great deal of attention to the study of love in churches. According to Erich Fromm, the reason we don't is that most people are concerned about the *object* of love instead of the *function of loving*.

Then too, many Christians tend to focus on the need and desire to be loved rather than on the need to love. But the love of God as a personal inner experience is participation in the actions of the Spirit of God. Love is acting. Love is the giving of oneself to another, the giving of one's heart and life. On the basis of a study by Daniel A. Prescott,[2] we might summarize the main psychological principles concerning love as follows:

1. *A person who loves enters more or less into the experience and feelings of the one loved.* This is called

75

empathy, a putting of oneself into the other person's shoes, seeing things from his point of view. Empathy also includes sympathy, a participation in the other person's feelings.

2. *One who loves is deeply concerned for the welfare and happiness of the loved one.* The Christian who loves has a *pastoral* concern. It was said of our Lord in prophecy: "He shall feed His flock like a shepherd." The Good Shepherd gave His life for His sheep. He gave *Himself* for us, "that those who live might live no longer for themselves but for Him who for their sake died and was raised." (2 Cor. 5:15)

3. *One who loves finds pleasure in making his resources available to the loved one and seeks to contribute as much as possible to the welfare and happiness of the loved one.* Love gives *for* as well as forgives. People in love want to share their lives, find pleasure in giving gifts to each other, and gladly help the one they love.

4. *On the other hand, the loving person accepts and respects the uniqueness and rights of the loved one, and allows him freedom of expression and self-determination to the degree that the relationship and the nature of the person permit.* There can be a prostitution of love. Some people use the *pretense* of love as their excuse for self-interest and self-gratification. We all know the parents who won't let go of their children under the claim that they love them too much to permit their freedom. Love can never be forced or imposed upon another and still be received as love.

Christians can happily note the amazing similarity between the love of God and the love that psychologists have recognized as creative, self-fulfilling, and productive, the basic force that provides wholeness and health in all aspects of life. It is a love that accepts and values any person unconditionally. This love affirms personhood and human life. It frees people instead of trying to possess and dominate and manipulate them.

EFFECTS OF LOVE

In his discussion of the effects of this kind of love, Prescott has pointed out that feeling unconditionally accepted and valued puts a person into a love relationship with the person who loves. When one feels loved and loves in return, says Prescott, it is easy to believe and do that which one's object of love believes and desires and does.[3] This identification and incorporation process is as fundamental in religious education as it is in psychotherapy.

Here we have a formula, an "open sesame," for dynamic entrance into another person's life and for bringing about desirable changes in an individual's thoughts, feelings, and behavior. Here is a basic design for education that is truly spiritual, effective, and self-propelling. Our trouble, in or out of the church, is that so few people practice this love, and even those who try do it so very poorly, including of course most of us.

But love is the only path by which God enters into the process of teaching. Therefore we teachers of religion in particular need to give foremost attention to the role of God's love in our teaching. We also need to consider what the functions of the teacher and the learning materials are in a communication process in which the love of God is the dominant spirit.

The role of the parent or teacher in a relationship of God's kind of love differs radically from the image of a person who doesn't communicate love. Anyone concerned about the spiritual life of another doesn't spout wisdom (his own or even God's) just to be

77

heard, nor does he try to "impress" or "drum" *his* knowledge and faith into another person.

Love changes the purpose, image, and function of the communicator. The teacher who loves sees himself as a pastor, a counselor and guide, a stimulator, a resource person, a helper, a servant—the opposite of a dictator, a boss, the "head" as he's called in England, or a master in the sense of a dominating ruler. The teacher who is like a spiritual father (or mother) deals with the *needs* of the individual or group, depends on the Word of truth for his power and influence, encourages a maximum of self-direction, helps the individual or the group use their resources (including other available people), and encourages genuine self-expression.

When the pervading spirit of the teacher is a desire to understand, accept, and further the welfare of the learner, then the role of the learning materials also changes radically from what it often has been and generally still is. The study or lesson materials become guides, resources, tools, *aids* to learning rather than subject matter to be taught simply because somebody apart from the actual teaching-learning situation decided it should be taught.

In a loving concern for the learner and the class as a whole, it is never the materials that are of first or final importance but the spirit and life of the learner—always. This does not lessen the need and value of prepared materials; it makes their use more purposeful and functional.

THE NEED OF PERSONAL CONCERN

But isn't the Word, the content, the subject matter bound to be neglected in such a system of Christian nurture? How can it be taught thoroughly without the pain of disciplined drill and study? These are fair questions, and they are important especially to people who believe in the Word of God as the means of grace.

We must agree that the Word, the message, the content, is always an essential part of the process of Christian communication and education, because without it there is no Christian communication. This principle was established in prior chapters, so let us not fall into sentimental secularism and emotionalism. But what we also must acknowledge, from another angle, is this: The Word, also the Word of God's love in Jesus Christ, becomes a meaningful revelation to the *receiver* only as the *Spirit* of the Word is seen and experienced by the learner.

Only as the receiver sees the relevance and applications of a Word to himself and to the worlds in which he lives will he chew and digest and thereby incorporate the Word into the fabric of his being and life. So there is not much point in communicating meaningless words or in trying to force-feed them, even if they are true and good and vitally important and even if they are words from the Bible itself. The importance of the Word is all the more reason why we must try to communicate it in the ways it is most likely to be received, understood, and taken to heart.

No one on earth has more reason to love than we Christians. In his first epistle St. John refers again and again to the kind of love God has bestowed on us, especially in sending His Son to be the remedy for our sins. Then he adds: "Beloved, if God so loved us, we also ought to love. . . ." (1 John 4:11)

It seems a shame, therefore, that recently the most articulate and loudest spokesmen for love in human relations were the hippies, who often reduced the meaning of the word to the lowest forms of irresponsibility and self-gratification. But as we are led by God, who is Love, to speak the Word of His love in love, we shall all become better witnesses of Christ and better teachers of His church and world. To that end we need to learn the *language* of God's Spirit.

The Language of the Spirit

Any kind of spirit, particularly also the spirit of love, is often more powerfully expressed and experienced in events and actions than by words. Furthermore, in the communication of spirit, *nonverbal* factors are at least as important and often *more* significant than the verbal elements. It's the old saying, "Actions speak louder than words," i. e., as vessels of truth, especially the truth of the spirit. We shall therefore look first at the language of spirit in human actions and living.

NONVERBAL COMMUNICATION

Almost all human behavior is indicative of a spirit and is therefore symbolic or symptomatic and meaningful. Happy laughter, for example, expresses a wholesome, congenial spirit. People who have little warmth of feeling or who hate intensely cannot laugh except in a cynical, derisive way. We don't call that a good laugh. Christians need to be able to laugh—at themselves and with others. It's a way of expressing love.

When experiences become very intense, they cannot even be expressed in words. Words fail us, we say, and we express our thoughts and emotions in awed silence. It is also difficult, if not impossible, for us to express our intimately *personal* thoughts and feelings adequately in words. For example, we can never quite communicate a sense of great joy just by telling about it; and an occasion that has inspired and moved us deeply is "just too much for words." In fact we sometimes find ourselves losing the spirit by talking about it. People deeply in love or in sympathetic grief often just sit and hold hands or look at each other in silence.

If the Christian faith were simply a matter of words and the church's task were merely the communication of words to the intellect, then all the latest developments in programed learning and machine teaching would be the church's best answer for carrying on its life and mission. The educational task of the church would be relatively simple; we could use propaganda and other conditioning methods and printed or recorded materials over and over again. But we can all readily see that such a procedure and its effects would be far from spiritual.

With the vast increase in verbal bombardments in the 20th century it is fortunate that modern man has become rather skeptical of words, spoken or written. They so often "don't mean a thing" because they don't really express the thoughts, feelings, and actions of the communicator. Parents, preachers, and teachers are prone to think of communication largely as verbal, but the psychiatrist has become very much aware of the fact that man speaks also through his behavior, just as God speaks through all His actions in and through people.

While acknowledging that written or spoken words often are needed to give clarity of meaning to nonverbal language, let us note (1) the great variety of action languages and object languages, and (2) the need of actions to establish the truth of our verbal messages.

1. To illustrate the first point, here are just a few of the many types of action languages that express thoughts and feelings even though they are not verbal: facial expressions, body postures and movements, gestures, vocal sounds such as coughs and screams, twitches and other tics, and our habitual behavior in general. Smiles, sighs, grimaces, gasps, a little wink or a twinkle in the eye (or the lack of it), the distance one keeps between himself and others, the direction of one's gaze—all these are very significant human communications.

We humans also express a spirit through the kinds of objects we create or keep around us and by the ways in which we use or display our possessions. The architecture of our homes and churches, the kind of furniture we prefer at home or tolerate in our church schools, the quality of art we like, the style of our clothing, our hair style, the kinds of books and magazines or the parts of the paper we read—all these reveal the spirits within us and among us.[4]

2. Some social scientists have called human behavior and culture "muted language" because it doesn't seem as direct and clear as verbal speech. But the principle that actions speak louder than words is evident in the fact that when our words do not agree with our actions, the truth of the *action* is communicated and not the message of the *words*. When we say to someone, "I'm always very happy to see you," but force a smile, glance at our watch, offer the person none of our time, and remain standing until the person leaves, the message of our *behavior* is communicated but not the meaning of our words.

So here we have another principle of communication: *When there is a discrepancy between words and reality, the truth in the reality of our thoughts, feelings, and actions is more likely to be communicated than the meaning of the words.* In this we have another working principle: *For effective Christian communication it is very important that the love of Christ be incorporated both in the inner spirit as well as outer behavior of the persons serving as the vessels of God's Word.*

"By this we know love," wrote John, "that He laid down His life for us; and we ought to lay down our lives for the brethren. But if anyone has the world's goods and sees his brother in need, yet closes his heart against him, how does God's love abide in him? Little children, let us not love in word or speech but in deed and in truth" (1 John 3:16-18). This indicates the necessity of loving also in the very *process* of communication, that is, in the act of communicating.

LOVING THROUGH DIALOG

As far as we can tell from the Gospel record, Jesus seldom used the lecture method, and never did He require a word-for-word repetition of His teachings or the teachings of the Bible. He was interested in getting people to *think* about their lives in relation to God, and to see and believe His Word for themselves. Today we say that Jesus was very *personal* in His communicating with people. In the next section we shall consider what this personal quality consists of. For helpful background let us first review briefly how the language of God's kind of love can be expressed in human *dialog.*

It's almost a ridiculous understatement to say that in recent religious education theory much has been said about dialog.[5] Though very few people in the church practice it (and hardly anyone is skillful at it), the word has become jargon along with a heap of other recent shibboleths. Too bad, because the system of communication known as dialog seems to be required by the Spirit of God. Let us see. We may later want to give it a different label.

What is meant by dialog? (We cannot assume that everyone knows the much-discussed but more often misunderstood meaning of the word.) Looking at its etymology, one could guess that the term refers to getting a word or message across (*dia* is the Greek preposition "through" or "across," and *logos* means "word"). But like most words, the word "dialog" has different levels of meaning. On one level dialog is simply two or more persons talking with one another—conversation and discussion. In a formal literary sense, it is written conversation.

But educationally the word refers to an interesting communication in which meanings of words and statements and concepts are explored, tested, corrected, and enriched by personal restatements and responses to restatements. In still another and more spiritual meaning, dialog involves communication of one's self and personal spirit with another person as a person—a communion of *persons* rather than communiques.

In *The Miracle of Dialogue* Reuel Howe defines the process as "that interaction between persons in which one of them seeks to give himself as he is to the other and seeks also to know the other as the other is."[6] Howe observed in a lecture at Concordia Seminary that man has two eyes, two ears, and only one mouth. This suggests, he said, that God intended us to use our mouth only half as much as our eyes and ears.

Genuine dialog requires listening to God and the other person in communication and places all the human parties in Christian communication under the Word of God as *He* speaks. This gives God a better chance to be heard. Furthermore, dialog that is prompted and directed by the love of God helps us actually love the people with whom we want to communicate. Thereby love does the teaching and changing of others.

The purpose of dialog is not simply to communicate *to* others, and never simply to *tell* them what to believe and do. The purpose is rather to help others make responsible decisions and responses of their own. Dialog therefore requires that a teacher see his pupils as persons to whom he can give himself rather than as persons to be ordered about, manipulated, coerced, brainwashed, and "formed" by his predetermination, self-will, force, or threat of force. It calls for the practice of faith (trust, firm reliance) in the workings of God's Spirit.

Furthermore, if communication as teaching is to *do* something to a person—if it is to result in personal changes of heart and mind and life—we must get into contact with the person or persons with whom we wish to communicate. First we need to establish a relationship, one that serves to open up the portals of the human spirit so that the Spirit of our Lord, the Redeemer, can enter to reign. Having established such a relationship by love, we must permit the Spirit of God to work from within the learner, setting off with sparks of His fire and the breath of His movements the personal understandings, motivations, and expressions of the other person as well as our own.

Again we need to remind ourselves that communication does not actually take place unless the message is *received;* also that learning involves changes *within the learner* — changes in thoughts, attitudes, and actions. As Professor Mayer acknowledged in his book *Interpreting the Holy Scriptures,* only when the Bible student is personally and emotionally involved in the Word under study does genuine understanding and learning take place.

TO GET AT THE WHOLE TRUTH

Reaction, interaction, and a free personal expression are essential to personal meanings and the personal experience of God's revelation. They also contribute to a true and deeper understanding of the *original* meaning of the written Word of the Scriptures. Almost any experience of what is called feedback shows us that both the original meaning as well as present meanings of a text can be misinterpreted or used without much depth — by the communicator as well as by the individual or group for whom the communication is intended.

When statements by either the leader or the group members can be questioned, clarified, or modified, dialog corrects misconceptions. By permitting free exploration, dialog also gives a *variety* of perspectives from various angles, thereby broadening and deepening the understanding of a truth under consideration.

For the Spirit to be able to lead us into all possible aspects of a truth, there must be some degrees of freedom for the Spirit to move people — within the limits of His truth, of course. This requires a somewhat different view of truth than many people have. Literalistic, legalistic, and dogmatic people (most of us, at times) maintain that a statement must be either true or false, while thoughtful reflection will reveal that many statements cannot be classified neatly as true or false. It depends.

In what is called the "Aristotelian" logic or way of thinking, red is red and can't be anything else, whereas in other ways of thinking different types and shades of red are recognized. In the more rigid way of thinking a person says, "John can't be both concerned and not concerned about the welfare of others." But the truth is that John may be very concerned about the welfare of his family while very little concerned about the welfare of his community or country.

Furthermore, to assume that we humans ever know the whole truth and nothing but the truth is a denial of our human shortcomings and the gravest of sins, because by this assumption we play God. Only *God* knows the *whole* truth of any matter. For this reason, too, we need to let God speak—by His Spirit in His Word—not only to us but also to those with whom we communicate; for our blindness, backgrounds, prejudices, and emotional needs invariably give a bias to our perceptions both of life and of God, and these affect our interpretations of God's Word.

Remember the parable of The Blind Men and the Elephant.

> It was six men of Indostan,
> To learning much inclined,
> Who went to see the elephant
> (Though all of them were blind).

In approaching the elephant each one felt a different part and in so doing got a different impression of this creature of God.

And so these men of Indostan
Disputed loud and long,
Each in his own opinion
Exceeding stiff and strong.
Though each was partly in the right,
They all were in the wrong!

The Spirit in Action

We shall now proceed to the more practical half of this course of study, though in the best sense of the word principles too are very practical. In the following sections we shall consider how the foregoing principles can be used, implemented, or carried out so that *God* dominates our communications and teaching. Somehow the teacher, the learner, the methods, and the materials must actually serve to *facilitate* the learning of the Word of God *in terms of His Spirit and life*. Otherwise they can be a hindrance or an interference to God's communications with the human spirit. This is why the second half of our study will be as important as the first half, if not more so.

5

The Spirit of the Lord speaks by me;
His Word is upon my tongue.

King David

2 Samuel 23:2

SPEAKING FOR GOD

At several points I called attention to the fact that content (in the formal sense of words, subject matter, and materials) is not the only medium of word and spirit. Also settings and their atmosphere convey moods and meanings; so do the purposes and attitudes of individuals and groups. All these factors either facilitate or hinder communication. As Karl Barth once said: "In a really living church there is perhaps nothing inconsequential at all." Everything in the church ought to speak the Word of God.

Especially the *human* communicator—the speaker, the leader, the teacher—is an important factor in communication. Usually our personal attitude and approach, more so than our words, determine the message and the spirit actually received by those with whom we communicate. The nature of the relationships, admittedly dependent in part on our actions in our relations, also determines to a great extent what we are able to communicate. Even Jesus was unable to teach the people who were prejudiced against Him and rejected Him. Let us therefore give some further attention to ourselves as communicators.

Persons Who Influence Others

We might think it unfortunate that God ordinarily uses people in communicating with people, but the most effective teaching of any subject takes place in *personal* communication. At the same time we must bear in mind that we speak for God by what we are and do as well as by what we say. Much as we may hate to admit it, messages and meanings are communicated also by human personality and behavior, not only by words.

In the past the study of the Christian as a person and as a teacher often was based on a list of what someone thought were desirable traits. We have all seen such checklists of personality characteristics for teachers: "A teacher must be cheerful. A teacher must be patient. A teacher must be well groomed. A teacher must be dedicated." The trouble is that most of the characteristics in such lists are debatable generalizations. There are times when a teacher should *not* be cheerful and patient, and people can be *too* well groomed and even too dedicated. (There is a loveless, proud kind of dedication that becomes work-righteousness.)

In any case, real interpersonal communication is possible only between real, truly spiritual persons. It may therefore be more helpful to ask what it means to be a real person and to consider briefly the nature of *realness* in people who are involved in any kind of communication, particularly that of teaching. (We shall not, of course, assume that every real person is necessarily a good teacher.)

ON BEING REAL [1]

As Paul Tournier and others have pointed out, all of us live to some degree behind a mask of convention, pretenses, habits, and false aspirations and motives. Tournier calls all these formalities our "personage." None of us can escape a personage altogether. Those who try doing so take on some peculiar airs of their own. We may as well live with the fact that we all have social obligations as well as the obligation to be ourselves.

Furthermore, we must recognize that no one is ever completely what he wants to be, no matter how hard he may try. Psychiatry has substantiated the words of St. Paul regarding the contradictory nature we all have: "I do not do what I want, but I do the very thing I hate. . . . For I do not do the good I want, but the evil I do not want is what I do. Now if I do what I do not want, it is no longer I that do it, but sin which dwells within me" (Rom. 7:15, 19-20). So we are all kept by sin and conditioning factors from being completely what we want to be.

But still this principle remains: The personality of the communicator plays a vital part in personal communication. And the teacher who is a genuine person is more likely to enter into person-to-person contact with his pupils than the person who is a phony. This leads us to the question of how a person can become more honest, more sincere, in order to become more real, more human, and more of a person instead of a personage.

We might first consider what is involved in being a real person. What's the difference between someone who strikes us as real and a person who gives us the uncomfortable feeling that something isn't ringing true? I once made a list of words descriptive of authenticity or genuineness and put terms for the opposite quality next to them. Both lists may serve as cues to what we're looking at:

authentic   inauthentic
genuine   artificial

honest	dishonest
true	false
real	phony
original	copy
human	mechanical
personal	impersonal

The next question I asked myself was, What would be some of the qualities of the people we would classify mainly on the right or on the left side of the list? We all are a little of both, of course, and sometimes we shift from one side to the other in differing situations; nevertheless, here are a few of the characteristics I noted. You may be able to add others:

spontaneous	forced
warm	cold
unaffected	affected
open	closed
unique	stereotyped
frank	deceptive
true	false
natural	unnatural

This still leaves us with the question of how we can become more real, more genuine, more truly human, more of a person and less of a personage —a follower and teacher of Jesus Christ, the Person "in whom is no guile" or pretense. "For realness," wrote Jacob Boehme, "the exterior of our life needs to be the signature of the interior." In one sense it always is, but when our exterior is a mask, it usually covers up what is underneath.

In order for me to be a real Christian person, nothing short of consistency between my profession of faith and my personal life is demanded. Since such

94

consistency is not completely possible, the real Christian is characterized by a spirit of genuine humility and repentance in which failings are readily admitted and the grace, forgiveness, and goodness of God are the mainspring of his heart and life.

Drawing on the bottomless well of living water available in the love of Christ, the real Christian is able to practice the love of God in his human relations, particularly also in teaching. Being a forgiven person, he can be honest with others and can forgive, accept, love, trust, respect, encourage, and enjoy them. Communicating with his students in the Spirit of Christ, the Christian teacher becomes a letter from Christ in his person as well as speech. In this becoming he receives the power to touch the spirit of others with the Spirit of God working through him.

This is why the faith and attitudes of the Christian parent or teacher are so essential to spiritual nurture and life. In Denmark and Sweden the teaching of the Bible and Luther's Catechism is prescribed by law, even on the secondary level, but this has not produced a nation of spiritually alive Christians. Why not? Very likely because many of the parents and teachers are not believing and practicing Christians themselves.

This suggests that though our realness as a person strengthens our influence on others, our personal involvement in the verbal Word of faith is vital too. Of course, with God all things are possible, and therefore His Spirit may be communicated in spite of the communicator being false or the communication being faulty. But ordinarily the Word of God becomes alive *through us* only as it is alive *in us*. This requires *our own insights* into the meanings of the Word and also our personal commitment to what we are communicating.

Assuming the principle that Christian communication, revelation, and spiritual nurture actually occur only when God acts in the communication, we still have the question, Under what conditions is the Spirit of God most likely to teach (that is, influence and change and direct) children, youth, or adults? More specifically, the question of this chapter is, How can one human being help another to receive God's Spirit and thereby learn to know God?

Previous sections acknowledged that the Word is essential as the means by which the illumination of the Spirit comes to be experienced. But human beings do not learn to know God in a truly spiritual sense simply by someone telling them Bible stories, drilling memory words, teaching formal statements of faith, and leading them in worship rituals and liturgical forms. If our ministry is to help others hear God speaking to them directly and personally — really hear His Word and thereby receive His Spirit — something more is required of us.

This does not say that the Word and Spirit of God are communicated in the neglect of the Scriptures and of Christian doctrine and liturgical forms, as some have foolishly concluded.[2] I repeat, what is needed is not something other than these, but a *comprehension* of these in fresh terms of contemporary human life and needs.

To help others gain such comprehension, we ourselves must translate, interpret, or transpose the historical Word to our own present lives, personal and social. In other words, as Gabriel Moran has shown much more fully,[3] for God to speak by His Spirit through the religious instruction of human beings, it is ordinarily necessary that we personally

96

and prayerfully *assimilate the meaning* of Scripture and "know the love of Christ which surpasses knowledge." (Eph. 3:19)

This requires that we not only put ourselves into the past events and situations and thereby participate in them, but we must also see for ourselves their parallels to situations, problems, questions, and issues in our own lives. *The Word must somehow speak to us personally before we can teach it meaningfully and with spirit to others.*

We must also be genuinely interested in actualizing the truths of the Word in our own lives and be concerned about others incorporating it into their lives. This is more likely to be the case when the focus of our attention is the Word in its present personal meanings and when the concern in communication is the relevant meanings for ourselves and for the learner. In other words, *the teaching task requires the drawing of parallels between the Word of the Gospel and life,* for ourselves as well as for those we hope to teach.

PERSONAL WITNESSING

Looking at the communication and teaching task in still another way, we might note that communication of the Word in the power of the Spirit calls for personal witnessing, but personal witnessing in quite a different sense than it often has in evangelistic talk and practices. In the revivalistic, "outreach" meaning of the word, it refers more to "winning" others for Christ and one of His church organizations than to a *teaching* of the Christian faith to others through the expression of personal experiences of God's love.

In the evangelistic understanding of the term, witnessing can easily become a deliberate, forced communication in which the will of the communicator

97

rather than the Spirit of God dominates both the message and the experience of it. Such stereotyped questions as "Brother, are you saved?" or admonitions to the unchurched to go to church and believe in Jesus Christ are not really personal *witnessing*. And the saying of what we have been told and trained to say is not necessarily *personal* witnessing, though it could be and no doubt also has been at times.

In any case we need to remember that God's Spirit comes only through a Word of Gospel and in the experience of love. But didn't Jesus say, "You shall be My witnesses" (Acts 1:8)? Yes, but to witness is to *teach*—by telling others (in any number of ways) the Word of Life that is Christ. And *personal* witnessing is sharing with others one's own experience of the grace and love of God available through faith in Jesus Christ.

Evangelistic witnessing too often amounts to "testifying" *about* Jesus, and to the "lost." This sets a barrier of distinction and separation between the communicator and the persons being addressed. *Personal* witnessing respects the freedom of all the parties in communication and permits a dialog in which the spirit of love can reign. Such a communication process is vital for the church as well as the world because it transmits the Word in present human terms that are more likely to seem alive and meaningful to the hearer.

"Bearing witness is the fundamental task of the teacher of religion," said Arnold Ingen-Housz.[4] By this remark he called attention to a profound difference between the teaching of religion and the teaching of any other subject. The teaching of a faith is not simply a matter of instructing others in a number of facts and truths. Because these truths involve attitudes and actions of life, the religion teacher must be concerned not only with their presentation; he must also give attention to the *effects* of the Word on the individuals and groups receiving and possessing it.

In such a view of teaching, the Christian teacher is not so much a person who "knows his stuff" and "instructs" others in what he thinks they *should* know. This he sometimes must do also. But in communicating with Christians, the teacher is a believer who feeds the flames of the Spirit of God already *within* others, and he does so in a mutual sharing-of-faith process. In Ephesians 4 the apostle Paul speaks of this communion of the Holy Spirit as a mutual edifying and building up of the body of Christ in love as *every* member of the body functions, not only the teacher.

In such a relationship of mutual faith the teacher bears witness to God by speaking the things he has heard and seen of Christ in the Scriptures. He also listens to what others have heard and seen. Far more than that, he speaks the heart of these things by *being* Christian, an image of God and of Christ, also in his communicating.

Though we are all imperfect images, we cannot truly witness and speak for God as a person without actualizing the Word in our person and personal contacts. In *The Trouble with the Church*, Helmut Thielicke emphasizes that what the preacher says in the pulpit must mesh with the rest of his existence in order to be convincing. The credibility of any witness for Christ depends not merely on his being imbued with a conviction that he is right, but on whether he lives "in the house of the dogmas he proclaims." [5]

99

Becoming an image of God in our living is more important to God's plan of salvation for the world than most of us want to admit. Statements of values and doctrines of faith can be taught to the intellect, and this has some effect. We do not deny this. But the principle to note here is that teaching *about* the love of God is not really heard unless it is also experienced, and it is more likely to be experienced when it is revealed in and by a person with whom we are in communion.

No amount of reading, hearing, or studying about a person will begin to give us the knowledge that the person's wife has of him, even if she cannot put what she knows into words. Because words alone fail to give us the deeply personal knowledge that one gains through living with a person, we need to live with God in order to introduce others to Him as a person and a spirit. Knowledge may bring about love, but it is even more true that the experience of love gives one knowledge. "The love of Jesus . . . none but His loved ones know," Christians sing in a popular hymn.

On Becoming More Personal

Thus far in this section I have tried to say that an experienced understanding of the Word is indispensable to a meaningful teaching of the Word. Far from diminishing the need for studying the objective word of the Scriptures, personal understanding requires serious reflection on it.

But personal knowledge is not something other than or added to knowledge. What is needed is *thoughtful* knowledge, the knowledge of personal experience and conviction. This kind of knowledge expresses itself in personal *witnessing*, not in a super-ficial, perfunctory, unrealistic, and sentimental use of fixed forms and formulations.

PERSONAL CORRESPONDENCE

The previous chapter introduced the need of dialog for an honest searching of the truths of the Sacred Scriptures and their spirit. Now we need to consider dialog once more as personal communication for the *transmission* of the Word and Spirit of God.

Most of us can recall a time when we said to ourselves, "That person really got to me!" or "Boy, that was great. I ate it up," just as the prophet Jeremiah ate the words of the Lord so that they became to him a joy and the delight of his heart (Jer. 15:16). What was involved in such an experienced communication?

We must stop fooling ourselves on the power of words as such. There can be a great and all-important difference between the saying of certain words by one person and the transmission of the identical words by another. This very real difference is illustrated by the way two people might play the same piece of music—"me" and a great violinist, for example.

But this difference, also in *effect*, is not a special gift that is limited to professionals or artists. Often a very simple expression of a young child or of an uneducated youth or adult touches us and causes our heart to respond.

Let's look at this matter first from the standpoint of *realness* in any kind of human communication. Somewhere I read about a man whose letters from his wife didn't reach him as he was traveling in the Orient. Meanwhile he was sending letters home regularly. Because his letters didn't reflect any

101

knowledge of the contents of his wife's letters (her remarks about their son's emergency operation, her questions about their income tax, her experience in wrecking their car), his letters seemed strange and perplexing to her, and she began to wonder whether he still cared at all about her and their children.

The qualitative difference between even a first-class business letter (whether it is falsely marked *personal* or not) and a genuine personal communication is evident in the contrast between an intimate love letter and correspondence addressed "To whom it may concern." The latter type is completely lacking in personal references, while the intimate message is filled with them. In an information bulletin the message is usually presented in matter-of-fact language to no one in particular. Only first-class personal communication is truly *cor*-respond-ence, meaning respondence from the heart (Latin: *cor*) to the heart.

To reach the heart of the person addressed, communication must be *co*-respondence and cor-*respond*-ence, that is, communication related to the persons addressed and to genuine responses from the other persons in the communication. Second- and third-class mailings seldom reflect the voice of the recipient even when they carry personal references to the writer and *his* relations and life. Most Christmas letters are of this type—and we all know how meaningless many of them are. Only first-class personal communications that relate directly to the recipient and reflect *his* voice are truly *correspondence*, heart-to-heart talk that moves a person to respond with his heart and spirit.

Some philosophers and educators have talked about this personal-correspondence type of communication as dialog. Teaching seen as dialog is more than a simple one-way communication of words. It is concerned, sympathetic, democratic, open, and free interaction between teacher and pupils rather than authoritarian pontificating or "stuffy" moralizing. It is mutual searching and sharing, the inclusion and participation of the learner in all phases of the learning process, rather than arid dictating.

The speaker or teacher who really gets to me is usually one who is interested in me, who wants to know what *I* think and how *I* feel and what *my* experiences have been, a person who respects me enough to listen to what *I* might have to say (also about God and His Word). He tries to put himself in *my* shoes and see what *I* think and say and feel and do from *my* point of view.

REAL TEACHING

In what is now a well-known article on what seems to facilitate the alteration of a person's spirit, character, and behavior, the noted American psychologist Carl Rogers summed up the present scientific evidence somewhat as follows:

1. It has been found that personal change is facilitated when the therapist is what he *is*, when in the relationship with his client he is *genuine*, without a "front" or facade, openly *being* the feelings and attitudes that at the moment are flowing in him. The more a person is able to listen acceptantly to what is going on within himself and the more he is able to *be* his feelings, without fear, the higher the degree of his integrity. When one says something he doesn't feel, when one "puts on" or plays a role without its proper feeling, even the tone of voice becomes incongruous and unconvincing.

2. When the therapist is experiencing a warm,

positive, and accepting attitude toward what is in the client, this too facilitates change in him. Such an attitude requires the therapist's willingness to let the client be whatever feeling is going on in *him* at that moment—fear, confusion, pain, pride, anger, hatred, boredom, love—whatever it might be. This acceptance means that the therapist values the other person in a total rather than in a conditional way. He doesn't accept a person when he is behaving in certain ways and reject him when he behaves in other ways. The term we have come to use for this is "unconditional positive regard."

3. The third condition for human change is called *empathetic understanding.* When a therapist is sensing the feelings and personal meanings the client is experiencing in a given moment and can perceive these from inside, as they seem to the client, and when he successfully communicates something of that understanding to his client, then this third condition is fulfilled. This kind of understanding is extremely rare. We usually offer an evaluative understanding from the outside—a judgmental understanding: "I understand. I too have had your experience." More empathetic remarks would be: "Are you saying—?" or "You seem to feel—. Am I right?" or "Do you mean—?" or "Am I correct in thinking that you—?" [6]

What Rogers says about a therapist applies equally well to any communicator and teacher. And his third principle indicates that even though genuineness on the part of both teacher and pupils is a prerequisite to real teaching and learning, there is the further question, How can one initiate and maintain the kind of dialog that serves as a means of entering into another person's life? What does the dialogical teacher do that the autocratic teacher does not do?

We have already gotten part of our answer from what we said about the nature of dialog or correspondence. For further clarification we might also look at a dialogical teacher in action. The teacher who is interested in fostering personal communication with his pupils usually can be characterized as one who (1) asks and deals with real questions, (2) listens encouragingly and helpfully to the students, and (3) fosters pupil initiative, participation, and creativity.

The first point requires what we have been saying: Our teaching must be relevant and significant *to the students*. In other words, the meanings of the Gospel must be addressed to the personal lives of the learners. To put it in still another way, the learners must be confronted individually with the Word; their individual lives must be related to the Word that is the lesson.

The second requirement of real teaching is not simply silence, because silence in itself could result in *loss* of contact and in pupil embarrassment and resulting perplexity or resentment. Nor does *helpful* listening consist in making friendly but insipid comments. The encouraging teacher helps the student say what he (the *student*) wants to say, and say what he means to say. This too calls for nothing less than the language of Christian love, the love that values with respect the other person as a person. It is a love that permits and even encourages differences of viewpoint and allows honesty and freedom to pervade under the Word of truth so that *the Word* can hold center stage and be heard.

The third characteristic of a teacher who desires

dialog is seen in his use of methods that foster pupil response, pupil participation, pupil-teacher and pupil-pupil interaction. It shows itself in planned opportunities for creative activities that permit individual and group expression of faith and spirit. Strangely enough, typical religious education makes little use of art and other creative activities as a medium of learning. In Chapter 8 I shall try to show how well all the arts can serve Christian education.

There is, of course, much more to be said on all these points and far more to be learned, but in this chapter I want to include one other noteworthy consideration. It lies in the fact that in really personal communication also our style of verbal language changes.

REALLY SAYING SOMETHING

Though normally we would not say that a person's speech is the person, still we can say that a person's language *reveals* the person to us. What he says and the way he says it expresses him. As the *logos* or Word of God gives us a true glimpse and revelation of what God is like, so also a human being's speech gives us some insight into his nature, being, and spirit.

Likewise the character of our own verbal speech may betray us and the true nature of our religion, our personal faith, and our feelings toward other human beings. So in spite of the predictions that we are moving into an age in which visual media and languages will be the most common mode of communication, we need to know what we can do with words and how we can best use words to communicate God's Spirit and love and life to others.

What makes some written or spoken language seem alive and some dreadfully dead? By looking

106

at examples of the use of words, we will perhaps see some of the previous considerations illustrated. We may also gain some additional understanding of the kind of verbal language most suited for communicating the Word with "power beyond words."

What is the matter with the following actually heard statements? Why would such use of words very probably *not* be convincing and inspiring, no matter how truthfully and well they were expressed? (1) "Oh, let Your ears be attentive to the voice of my pleadings." (2) "Christians are so dear to one another that it makes them sad to part." (3) "We must do the right and shun the wrong." (4) "The cause we espouse is a right cause, so we must persevere and not falter, though others may seek to allure us from the beaten path on which we try to win precious souls for heaven."

Or consider the flavor of these "religious" statements: (5) "Your heart is black with sin." (6) "The Evil One has been sowing some seed in your heart." (7) "We need to reach out for the lost and win sinners to Jesus." (8) "Isn't it a privilege to be engaged in the salvation of souls?" (9) "It behooves us to eschew things contrary to our profession."

No doubt anyone could easily find his own examples of "evangelistic," churchy, sentimentally pious, archaic, stereotyped, phony, meaningless statements, language that is plainly not religious even though it is used for religious purposes. It won't really hurt to become painfully aware of the dead language we all thoughtlessly use. It's the only way we'll get rid of some of it.

What then are some of the important considerations in our use of words for the communication of God's Spirit and life? In a very instructive article on

107

religious language, F. H. Drinkwater says: "Everybody admits, of course, that the language we use should be simple, but perhaps we don't always realize *how* simple."[7] He then goes on to show that many frequently used and familiar words (like the word "divine") may *seem* simple but are quite meaningless to most adults as well as children, especially when used in a religious reference.

But the need for simplicity and clarity is not solved by the use of short and commonly used words, as advocates of Basic English have assumed. A girl knows very well what her boy friend means when he says, "You look simply divine!" On the other hand, who knows what is meant when we say, "The soul of education is the education of the soul"?

The key to a language that speaks clearly to the heart, says Drinkwater, is in an appeal to the imagination. He calls this language poetic, as opposed to scientific or technical language. He also recognizes that both poetic and technical language can be either simple or difficult. But only a poetic-simple language of ordinary life, he maintains, communicates a sense of the supernatural and can carry a power that reaches the heart.[8]

What then are the characteristics of ordinary-simple-poetic speech? Language students have pointed to some of the features of words that convey thought with the power of a spirit. Powerful, moving, captivating language is "characteristically personal," sincere language "straight from the heart." Often it is "logically odd" or paradoxical, also full of metaphors and other figures of speech.

Interesting writing or speech doesn't try to "spell it all out" but leaves something to the imagination. It points to eternal truths of life through natural signs and symbols that may have more than one meaning. One can see this kind of language in almost any folk song and in many popular songs of the day. Recently my 7-year-old was singing happily:

> She makes me laugh,
> She makes me cry.
> She flies like a bird
> In the sky—yigh-yigh.
>
> Oh me, oh my,
> See how I sigh.
> Now I know
> I can't let Maggie go.

We can easily see the simplicity of the language, the personal nature of the verse, the strong reference to feelings, the vivid seeing of Maggie as a bird in the sky. Such words are naturally appealing, readily learned, richly expressive, happily remembered.

In looking at folk songs, the reader will become amazed at how simple but full of symbols they usually are: "Michael, row the boat a-shore. Allelujah!" "Where have all the flowers gone?" "How many times must a man look up before he can see the sky? How many ears must one man have before he can hear people cry?"

Ian Ramsey said that this kind of symbolic language leads to "life by a thousand enrichments" rather than to "death by a thousand qualifications." It speaks through parables and analogies that give a self-involving "onlook" instead of merely presenting literal, bare, and dry facts by means of technical terms, definitions, and "purely objective" statements.[9]

This dynamic figurative language is what the inspired writers of the Bible and Jesus Himself so often used. Of our Lord it is written: "Indeed He said nothing to them [the crowds] without a parable"

(Matt. 13:34). And the prophet Ezekiel, when asked to speak for God, said: "Ah, Lord God! They are saying of me, 'Is he not a maker of allegories?'" (Ezek. 20:49)

This kind of symbolic language we need to use in speaking for God. What this means and how this principle applies to teaching for God will be indicated in the chapters that follow.

6

Those who live according to the Spirit
set their minds
on the things of the Spirit. . . .

You are in the Spirit
if the Spirit of God really dwells
in you. . . .

The Spirit Himself intercedes for us
with sighs too deep for words.

St. Paul

Romans 8:5, 9, 26

6

LEARNING THROUGH THE SPIRIT

Any Christian communicator (parent, preacher, teacher, writer, artist) is a person who speaks for God. He is a minister (servant) of the Word in the functioning sense of the term. But we must keep in mind that the Word in reality is a person, a spirit, and a way of life. The understanding of this Word requires something more than verbal, intellectual definitions, explanations, and instructions. Though these are needed too, spiritual meanings of the Word must be *experienced* through the experience of the *Spirit* of the Word.

As we move now to a consideration of the *other* persons in communication and their ways of learning, I hope to show how learning by an experience of revelation (or by the experiences that give one a revelation) depends on the action of a spirit within the spirit of the learner. The purpose of this section of our study will be to make us more aware of how Christian faith and life and its nurture actually are dependent on the workings of God's Spirit, as we Christians confess but often fail to believe.

Christian learning is a happening between God and the learner, with other people involved only instrumentally — as helpers, who may even hinder. Anyone who thinks he can decide with absolute certainty to teach some other person and assumes that he can determine what the person will learn has a misleading opinion of his role. In fact he misconceives the entire process of Christian education.

This is evident also in the fact that only the *learner* learns, and what the learner learns from what he is taught or teaches himself depends, among other things, on the kind of person he is—his background, his attitudes, his involvements. The assumption that the student learns what the teacher teaches is obviously more often false than true. In the words of an old axiom, "Whatever is received is received according to the manner of the one receiving it."

Furthermore, learning is something the learner *does*. In actual learning the learner is active, not passive. Also in the experience of divine illumination, conversion, sanctification, etc., there is a human participant who *actively* receives the gift and gifts of God's Spirit, though the initiative and power come from God. This human response of participation is not always in conscious awareness (as in the case of an infant receiving the life of God in Holy Baptism); nevertheless, a person's growth in the Christian faith and life requires the development of conscious personal understanding and deliberate, free decisions and choices.

In view of these self-evident facts, it is folly to assume that communication and teaching consist mainly in saying words to others. In reality communication consists in what is heard or discovered and taken to heart, and successful teaching depends on what a lesson does to the student and what the learner does with the lesson. Consequently, the church needs teachers who think of their ministry in terms of the learner and actual learning.

What We Know About Learning

The influence of settings, personal relations, and the spirit of a person's group and community have already been noted. Previous sections also called attention to the need of genuine dialog and a currently alive language if learning through a communication is to be spiritual. Repeatedly I have mentioned, too, the importance of relevant and personal interpretations of content.

In addition to these understandings of how a person comes to possess a faith and spirit, what can we learn about learning from scientific studies? The following principles have been rather reliably established and are generally accepted by informed psychologists and educators.[1] It would therefore be unwise on our part to ignore these findings:

1. A person's background, assumptions, attitudes, needs, perceptions, and motivations play a distinct part in what he hears, sees, learns, and thinks in any teaching-learning event.

All of us know what entirely different thoughts we have privately than most people *assume* we have while they are speaking to us. Even when our thoughts are related to what is being said to us, they are always somewhat different from another person's thoughts on the same subject. Genuine personal learning is individually unique, as anyone can demonstrate if he will encourage the students to express what *they* see, think, and feel.

Only through response and critical evaluation of expressions is there a safeguard against misconceptions. Only through "talkback" does a communicator receive any assurance that the learner is getting the idea, the truth of the matter, or that he

115

is getting anything at all out of the communication. Through sharing and exchange of thought, the understanding of the teacher as well as the learner is both enriched and corrected.

2. Learning of any kind is reinforced and strengthened when it is rewarded. The reward is most effective if it is directly connected with the expressing or doing of what is to be learned. On its lowest level this main principle of so-called behaviorism, drawn from literally thousands of experiments with animals, leads to some highly questionable practices. When human learning is reduced to mere recall of drilled words and given answers or the doing of trained or instructed responses for the sake of rewards, then people are treated as animals and not as intellectually and spiritually endowed creatures of God.

Material rewards and awards (stars, grades, pins, gifts, certificates, etc.) may have some value in strengthening contact with children or adults. Their spiritual value depends on how they are used. But they aren't really needed and worth the trouble when the power of the spirit is strong—least of all with young children, who are the greatest in the spiritual kingdom of heaven. Fortunately most churches and church schools do not resort to green stamps, and most teachers of religion are not burdened with systems of grading.

On the other hand, the finding that rewards strengthen learning is most applicable but unfortunately less applied to *higher* types of learning and higher types of rewards. By higher we mean the intrinsic rewards of pleasure and satisfaction, of accomplishment and self-fulfillment, that come to a learner *immediately* through the experience of a spirit and in direct connection with what is learned. For

116

self-perpetuating and significant learning, the law of learning by reinforcement requires rewarding experience within the learner's mind, heart, spirit.

3. Readiness for new learning is partly a matter of physical and psychological maturation, but it also depends on the learner (1) sensing in the new learning a value for him and his world, (2) seeing a fair chance of being able to learn what is being taught and expected, and (3) feeling a freedom from compulsion or threat.

By now there are several internationally known studies of readiness for learning that have focused directly on the moral and religious development of children and youth.[2] We cannot consider here all the findings that a course in the development of the human mind and person might review, but let us note that teachers of religion cannot blithely or piously assume, as many have, that all Bible or other religious material will benefit people at any age.

Nor can we maintain that all religious content can be made meaningful to human beings at any stage in their development. A study of 800 American children (Roman Catholic, Protestant, and Jewish) over a period of 5 years indicated that before the age of 11 or 12 children are unable to understand religious concepts as they are understood by adults. To handle this problem they spontaneously give their own meanings to religious terms beyond their comprehension.

Because a child is most like adults in his feelings and least like them in his thinking, David Elkin concluded that for children religious education ought to deal primarily with feelings and actions.[3] This, of course, does not suggest the elimination of doctrines and concepts, but it does emphasize the

117

importance of giving emotional, active experiences of religious truths instead of abstract presentations, particularly to young children.

OTHER CONDITIONS FOR LEARNING

4. Learners tend to progress in a certain direction only as far as needed to achieve their purposes or fulfill their need. For this reason I once wrote an article on "What Do You Expect of Your Pupils?"[4] In it I called attention to the conviction of psychiatrists that a patient can begin to think of a fundamental reeducation of himself only after he is convinced that his neurosis brings with it a living death.

In Christian nurture, too, the learner needs an awareness of the living death that lies in separation from God. He must become convinced that learning to know God is really a matter of life and death. He must see the vital necessity of being in touch with God and transformed by His Spirit in order to enjoy the life eternal.

A second prerequisite in psychotherapy is that the patient must have not only the desire for but also the expectation of help. He must have hope of salvation. The patient who is so crushed and depressed that he is in despair is a poor risk. Studies of the effects of placebos (inactive medicines) on patients suggest that one of the features accounting for some of the success of any form of medical treatment is arousing the patient's expectation of help and attaching that hope to a particular object or event.

In Christian nurture the law of God must be used for developing an ongoing awareness of the need of salvation and a transformed life with God. But always the emphasis needs to be on the positive Gospel promises of God's love and blessings in

118

order that hope may burn brightly in the pupil—hope for the bountiful, eternal life Jesus said He came to give. The Law, the surgery of cutting criticisms, or what is called the reality principle (the facing up to the facts of one's life), can be highly destructive unless the judgments of God are used sensitively and lovingly.

A third type of expectancy considered vital in psychotherapy is the patient's perception of the therapist as a person with power to help. Also in education the student must have a basic respect for the teacher as one who can and will help him. And the therapist too must believe that he is able to help the patient. "We must believe in what we are doing," is a motto often voiced by doctors and psychiatrists.

Likewise teachers must believe that their pupils can be helped. The child who feels that the teacher has given up on him is doomed to failure. Christian parents and teachers in particular have reason to believe in the worth and potential of every human being because they can believe in the redeeming power of God. When a student feels that the teacher has a wholehearted, steady, active interest in his development, his own aspirations, efforts, and accomplishments are more likely to rise.

5. It has been demonstrated that young children, youth, or adults are more likely to throw themselves into a learning activity if they themselves have participated in the selection and planning of it, are convinced of its value, are committed to its purpose, and feel free to pursue the matter in their own way.

In other words, the learner's genuine participation all along the line furthers his learning. Arbitrary and forced direction by the teacher or any group leader, especially when excessive, is likely to result in apathy, a ready conformity, defiance, sabotage, dragging of heels, or some other mode of escape from the whole business. No doubt the reader can easily conjure up his own examples.

What reasons do the students of your church school have for coming? Without prejudging them, it might be sobering to find out. Do they come out of a sense of duty or habit, or because of family pressures? What do they expect to get out of coming? A sense of spiritual need and some experienced hope of answers to this need are necessary motivation. It deserves whatever time is needed for its development. Much time is wasted by trying to teach individuals or groups that are not ready to be taught because of their attitudes.

When they come, are the students kept aware of the purpose of the program (namely learning and change)? Do those who attend the classes agree to give their attention to what is to be learned? Do they think of themselves as members of the church, responsible for helping one another grow in the Christian life? The teacher who comes to common purposes with his pupils and then keeps the class members mindful of them is bound to be more successful than one who tries to teach others without their commitment to the learning task.

6. One more point: We learn by thinking, and this principle applies equally to religious education. Especially learning that is to become actual through insight produced by the Spirit involves concern, not simply dumb, silent assent. Concern calls for personal decisions, commitment, responses, obedience, willing sacrifice, and dedicated service. Recently the term for all this has been "personal involvement."

But one cannot put his heart into something he

hasn't thought about or thought through. So another question we need to ponder is, How can we stimulate the learner to *think*? What conditions and methods lead to thinking? How much thinking do we and the church in general permit or, better yet, require—of children or adults? How much Christian thinking actually goes on in *your* home, *your* class, *your* parish? Why isn't there more of it? Why is so much religious education quite obviously not thought provoking?

Paul Tillich said that one of the main reasons religious education is usually dull and uninspiring is that it must give answers to questions children and youth have not asked.[5] But if such answers fall on deaf ears, why give them, no matter how important they are? Why not wait until the questions have been raised, and why not start with questions the learners already have or can be led to ask for themselves? We can't teach everything at any given time and need not, for that matter.

Human beings are more inclined to think when they encounter a problem or are faced with a real question, an issue, an intellectual challenge that involves them and therefore interests them. To stimulate thinking we must ask *real* questions, questions that are real to the learner, issues of life in their present, concrete, personal, and social lives, not just fact questions with obvious answers.

If we truly want the other persons in communication to think and not simply to tolerate or parrot our thinking, what must we do? A book that presumes to offer all the answers also inhibits the thinking of the reader. For this reason all the suggestions in this book must be taken only as information, concerns, a viewpoint, and possibilities to be considered by the reader. After a question is explored,

121

personal evaluation of the findings (through reading, observations, experiment, and thinking) must follow.

A popular paperback by Eric Hoffer titled *The True Believer* gives a far-from-flattering picture of a true disciple.[6] The true believer is seen as a fanatic who is helplessly obsessed and blindly driven by a faith that has spiritually enslaved him. Christian parents, leaders, and teachers are interested in their children becoming true disciples of Jesus Christ and true believers in Him. But as we shall see in the second section of this chapter, such persons are *free* in spirit, not brainwashed, conditioned automatons who give the right answers and do expected behavior when buttons are pushed by someone else.

The true disciple of Christ has a personal faith, a personal communion with the triune God through His Word and Spirit acting within his very own mind, heart, soul, self, or spirit—call it what you will. The word "disciple" itself suggests a learner who by the discipline of learning becomes a genuine (true) follower of another person, a believer in his teachings. But personal faith and self-discipline do not develop apart from personal reflection and understandings, a personal interest in the life meanings of the Word of faith, and personal responses to the Spirit of God.

The nurturing of such an inner faith within the spirit of the learner does not call for *less* teaching of the Word or *less* concern with intellectual knowledge and more attention to feelings and experiences as such. Rather it demands a relating of the learner's heart and life to the Word and requires his thoughtful study of the Word in relation to himself and the real worlds in which he lives.

We teachers of religion too often forget that faith is truth in the *inward* parts. It is an understanding and wisdom of the Spirit *within the heart or spirit of the learner*. It is more than assent to or acceptance of the teachings of the Bible and of a church body. We have always acknowledged this theologically. But our interest has too seldom been in the learner's personal decisions regarding the truth of the matter being taught. And too little have we encouraged responsive, self-directed lives of Christian faith.

At a time when people are living in a wide-open society that no longer can be controlled by traditions and other external forces, the development of the self-directing capacities of human beings has become crucial for the church as well as the world. We never could and no longer dare assume that the kingdom of God comes through what we do outwardly to people or with them. We cannot "make" Christians by enrolling them in church programs and organizations and by "confirming" them in the Christian faith through a ceremony.

Because the life of God's kingdom is within people, we must shift our focus from words and formulations and prepared materials and machinery to the spirit of the learner. We need to give more attention to the learner's own understandings and his own real life and behavior. We need to provide much more occasion for experiences of Christian faith on the part of those whose spiritual development we want to further. And we must want and must expect *honest* personal expressions of faith and the *doing* of the Christian faith.

In discussing the general need of fostering self-direction for citizenship in our modern world, Arthur Combs listed some of the public education practices that mirror the belief that learning is chiefly the acquisition of factual knowledge: preoccupation with right answers, cookbook approaches to learning, overconcern with rules and regulations, preoccupation with materials instead of with people, single approaches to learning, emphasis on remembering rather than on understanding and skills, greater attention to details than to principles.[7] Isn't all this frightfully characteristic also of religious education, which ought to deal with the life of the spirit?

Learning is a personal matter, individually unique and dependent on the cooperation of the learner. Giving students the information they could get by themselves and requiring set answers is not, therefore, the best way to help others toward a genuine faith of their own. And only a personal, responsible, self-directing faith can meet the tests of life in the kind of world that appears to be ahead of us. It's the only kind of faith that ever was truly moral and religious.

How, then, can personal responsibility and self-direction be fostered also among Christians? Arthur Combs suggested that we must first believe in the importance of self-direction and then give the learner more opportunities to practice self-direction. "Education," he said, "must be seen not as providing right answers, but as confrontation with problems; not imaginary play problems either, but *real* ones in which decisions count."[8]

This kind of education calls for a much greater use of the methods we shall consider in the remaining two chapters. These methods also require a high degree of freedom, more freedom than most children, youth, or adults experience in their churches and church schools.

Learning to Be Free

"Where the Spirit of the Lord is, there is *freedom*," wrote the Spirit-inspired St. Paul (2 Cor. 3:17). Though he was referring specifically to spiritual enslavement under the law of Moses, he also wrote about "the glorious liberty of the children of God" and of all creation in the whole life of the Spirit of God (Rom. 8:19-23). And "the Lord [Christ] who is the Spirit" (2 Cor. 3:18) said, "The truth [My Word] will make you free." (John 8:32)

Now, what is this freedom that the Holy Scriptures say is in the very nature of God and of all truly spiritual life? This is another subject of capital importance. Many books have been written about it. It is beautifully illustrated in the parable of the Prodigal. To review the Christian Gospel of salvation from what the Bible calls sin and the demands and judgments of God's laws, one need only read the Letter to the Galatians. It clearly presents the perfect Spirit and life of freedom that any person may freely enjoy in a responsive relationship to God through faith in Jesus Christ.

In glowing terms Paul writes of the Christians who have entered into a life of forgiveness and love through faith in Jesus Christ. He speaks of them as redeemed "from the curse of the Law . . . no longer under a custodian . . . no longer a slave but a son, and if a son then an heir. . . . For freedom Christ has set us free," Paul booms out after his discussion of the matter; "stand fast, therefore, and do not sub-

125

mit again to a yoke of slavery. . . . For you were called to freedom." (Gal. 3:13, 25; 4:7; 5:1, 13)

Again we acknowledge that the apostle is referring primarily to freedom from Old Testament laws and human regulations, but then the letter goes on to say that this is a freedom to love and serve one's fellow human beings. It is a freedom to live by the Spirit of God, not a freedom to indulge in what Paul calls the desires of the flesh and of the elemental spirits. Spiritual freedom is not license to do what one pleases or simply what one thinks he *must* do, such as the "beggarly" Old Testament regulations the Jews had to follow prior to the coming of Christ.

In Christian education we are concerned with the learning through the Spirit of God alive in human love, joy, peace, patience, kindness, self-control, and all other Christian virtues. Our point here is that these cannot be taught by telling people what they should do or by asserting laws and exerting pressures of any kind.

This is, strangely enough, the hardest lesson to learn even though it is at the heart of the Christian faith. How often we think we can change people and "make" them Christian (or at least better) by scolding, moralizing, manipulating, or regulating them.

FREEDOM THROUGH LOVE

Because the Spirit of God revealed in Jesus Christ is the Spirit of freedom as well as of love, *the life of the Spirit cannot be experienced except in freedom.* If only we could believe this! Strangely enough, often the more outwardly religious and zealous we become, the more we sin against this spiritual principle.

How then does the freedom of God's Spirit find

expression (how is it actualized and realized) in human relations and life? What are some of its dynamics, and how does it affect human relations and interpersonal communications?

There are many different concepts of freedom, just as there are many different concepts of love. We are concerned here with *God's* kind of freedom, the freedom of His Spirit as it affects and transforms the human spirit. God's freedom is inseparable from His love because they are both qualities of one and the same Spirit.

We might, therefore, profitably take another look at the great "love chapter" in the Bible (1 Corinthians 13) and note how God's Spirit calls for freedom in communicating His love to others. In fact, we shall see that freedom is the only medium through which the communication of love can take place.

Let us note how Paul describes the love of God in action: "Love is patient and kind; love is not jealous or boastful; it is not arrogant or rude. *Love does not insist on its own way* [not even in teaching religion]; it is not irritable or resentful; it does not rejoice at wrong but rejoices in the right. Love bears all things, believes all things, hopes all things, endures all things" (vv. 4-7). Here is a spiritual basis for freedom. Without love there is no real spirit of freedom, just as there can be no love without freedom.

We do not love when we are prejudiced and intolerant, when we are narrowminded and closed to other people's viewpoints, when we are proud and think that our knowledge and ways are superior to others, when we insist on our way of seeing, saying, and doing things. To underscore the freedom that lies in love, the apostle added: "Love bears all things, believes all things, hopes all things, endures all things" (v. 7). Just think of what that might mean — and of how little anyone practices it!

FREEDOM IN EDUCATION

To see that love requires freedom for the learner, especially also in religious education, we need to consider briefly what it means to act in a spirit of love and therefore to bear, believe, hope, and endure all things. Bearing means "putting up with," but it also means more than that. When Paul said, "Bear one another's burdens, and so fulfill the law of Christ" (Gal. 6:2), he was talking about becoming involved in a responsible, helpful relationship with others.

Likewise, believing all things must be understood as an attitude and spirit, but it's something more than "looking for the best in people" or "putting the best construction on everything." It's a believing in people because of what God can do with them and through them when He works in them.

Similarly hope is an anticipation of an improved future condition. Hope, said Gabriel Moran, is to look on a person with the eyes of God.[9] A parent or teacher who despairs of a child destroys the very process by which the child might be saved.

And finally, said Paul, love is in the enduring of all things. It prompts us to carry on under the stresses and troubles of life instead of running away from them. When the other person is difficult, when a class makes life unpleasant for the teacher, when children and adolescents are a problem, we are all tempted to give up trying to communicate with them in order to help them. Only the spirit of love gives us the power to endure.

To translate these principles of love into our communications with others requires a trust in the Spirit

128

of God at work *in the other person,* child or adult. We Christians believe that all who receive the Word of God's forgiving love in Christ Jesus, whether through the sacraments or the words of the Gospel, have a measure of God's Spirit within them. Love and current theories of human development require that we put our faith in God's power into our teaching by allowing God's Spirit and His truth to work freely within the learner.

Leaving the results of Christian communication and education to God not only leads to the kind of witnessing role we considered previously; it also suggests dialog in which the other persons in communication are respected as having some unique understanding of God and His Word because they have received the Spirit of God through His Word. As William Hulme has pointed out, only this view gives to all Christians their rights and responsibilities as children and priests of God.[10]

The placing of trust in the workings of God's Spirit within the spirit of the learner necessitates a vital concern that the Word of God is really communicated by the use of whatever method is used for teaching and learning. Such concern lessens the temptation of the communicator to depend on his personality or presentation for his influence and results. It makes the Word the only authority and power instead of the teacher. Focus on the Word also guards the learner against becoming lost or tied up in the mechanics of a learning activity instead of being engaged by its substance and spirit.

But only in a teacher-disciple relation of love do both parties enter substantially into the Word of God together. And only in freedom can the disciple gain an honest, genuine, authentic faith of his own. For

129

only as we feel free to think for ourselves and say what we really think (also when we disagree) do we become open to changes of mind and heart. This is true of all people, including our students.

VALUING HUMAN UNIQUENESS

One more related point: The love that breathes freedom not only values the individual but also values his individual uniqueness. This principle too has great bearing on the kinds of methods and materials to be considered in the remaining two chapters. Every individual — child, youth, or adult — is not only a unique person; he also has unique talents and potentials for what he might become and do creatively.

Even though Jesus spoke of these talents in sets of one, five, and ten, He wasn't implying that all who receive one talent get the *same* talent or that all who receive ten have the same ten. "There are varieties of gifts," is the way St. Paul put it. "In each of us the Spirit is manifested in one particular way, for some useful purpose." (1 Cor. 12:4, 7 NEB)

In today's world the church and its leaders and teachers must learn to value and foster the *uniqueness* of every human being. While churches as a whole are noted more for their interest in conformity (this is not to be confused with unity), especially the younger generations have little patience with any kind of pressures to conform, and understandably so. They are fighting desperately against becoming the anonymous man, the mechanical man, the organization man, or the computerized man in an age of mass media, growing technology, population explosion, and concentration of business and political power in the hands of a few.

God loves people as *individuals*, as individual

persons, "calling them all by name" (Is. 40:26). The church's message is that God loves the individual as did the shepherd who left his 99 sheep and went looking for the one that was lost. The Spirit of God, who is Love, not only accepts, values, and seeks to serve every individual as a unique person; His love also allows the individual the freedom to be what he is and to become what he might become under the grace of Christ.

Life that is common, stereotyped, and lacking in originality becomes dull, empty, meaningless, spiritually dead. So one might expect that we Christians, of all people, would be fostering and enjoying *differences* within the boundaries of God's Word and Spirit.

But what is the strange actuality that one can see in almost any parish program, especially in its ministry of the Word? And what are the expectations of most Christian parents, teachers, and leaders? What kind of student do we appreciate? The one who thinks for himself and expresses God's truth and spirit in his own inimitable ways? Or the one who gives pat answers, the answer in the book, the party line? Too often in the church there seems to be a demand for a deadening conformity instead of a preference for the unique products of God's creative Spirit. It doesn't have to be that way, and we can help change the picture.

If the church will foster and cultivate a growing interest in people as individual persons and will treat its students as marvelously unique creations of God, she will readily find growing opportunities to fulfill her mission—that of giving life to human beings, the abundant life that the Lord of the church said He came to give (John 10:10). This I believe! In fact, this I know from experience and have no doubt about.

*No one puts new wine
into old wineskins. . . .
But new wine
must be put into fresh wineskins.*

Jesus

Luke 5:37-38

METHODS FOR A MINISTRY
TO THE SPIRIT

I can hear voices saying, "At last we've come to something practical—*methods*, the subject we should have been studying all along." But haven't we been considering procedures for communicating the Word of God in the power of His Spirit? That's a question of methods! Well then, what now? In this chapter we will be thinking further on the foregoing principles but will consider them more directly in the form of techniques.

The purpose of any method used in Christian education is to bring human beings into communion with God. This applies to baptized Christians already in His kingdom as well as to non-Christians. Such a purpose makes methods important—not relatively unimportant, as many people in church education seem to think. Any method is subordinate to its task and function, but so is all content. The question of methods, therefore, is no *less* important than other considerations in Christian communication. Nor is the study of methods practical as opposed to theological, and therefore a matter that can be disdained or ignored.

Methods are inseparably related to the mission of God and the teaching ministry of His church. Instead of being of such secondary importance that it doesn't matter much *how* we teach as long as the content is right, methods or procedures help determine the spirit and meaning of our communications. Sometimes our message is in the way we communicate rather than in the materials or other media we use or in what we say. More often than not the method at least affects the meaning of the message.

So let us look seriously at our methods of communicating for the purpose of educating. Let us try to learn from our foregoing principles what our practices need to be. What kind of methods ought we to use for a ministry to God and human beings? What kind of communicating and teaching procedures would serve God's purposes best in our parish, in our church schools, and in our own teaching of the Christian faith?

To be willing and able to learn the right answers to these questions requires an honest consideration of what we are doing. This is necessary, though painful, especially if we are unconsciously in disagreement with the foregoing principles in our ways of teaching if not also in our thinking.

The Way Teaching Is

A few years ago the Center for the Study of Instruction of the National Education Association in the United States published a report titled *The Way Teaching Is*. In it Philip Jackson said: "At present the dominant *Geist* is to view teaching as though the teacher's task were principally to produce specific changes within the student; as though, in other words, there were an intimate and direct relation between teaching and learning."[1]

Even though Christian learning is inner change and modification of behavior, our basic principle has been that such learning is dependent on the

Spirit of God working through the Word of God. An accent on specific changes through what the communicator does can lead to all kinds of false notions and harmful practices that keep God from doing the educating. In efforts at teaching specific behavior instead of the Word, which is the necessary seed and food of the Christian spirit and life, another form of legalism may readily appear.

Principles of faith and life can, of course, be very specific. Jesus said pointedly, "Love your neighbor as yourself," "love your enemies," and forgive seventy times seven times. And the apostle Paul gave long lists of specific actions for instruction in righteousness. But these are all a Word or principle.

Our concern is that in teaching specific applications of principles, we may make them laws instead of keeping them as illustrations under certain circumstances. For example, the emphasis in Christian education for the very young on sharing cookies or helping Father rake leaves or doing the dishes for Mother can easily become moralizing. Somehow the connection between the concrete examples of life and the principle or Word of faith must be kept.

The influence of a spirit on a person may not necessarily occur in the presence of a teacher or in a classroom. It may happen in altogether different times and forms than that which was designed by the curriculum writer or the lesson planner. (This doesn't deny the value and need of planned materials and lesson planning. The principle simply "rights" our concerns.) Jesus said: "The kingdom of God is as if a man should scatter seed upon the ground. . . . The earth produces of itself, first the blade, then the ear, then the full grain in the ear." (Mark 4:26, 28)

There are many other common and perhaps

137

questionable conceptions of the educational process, all of which have found their way also into Christian religious education. They could be grouped in various ways, but here are a few mentioned at random: Education has been called and thought of as—

handing down a heritage (transmitting or impressing a subject matter).

"bringing up" children (molding, directing, guiding, forming, raising).

nurturing and training (feeding and disciplining).

ministering to (helping, enabling, tutoring).

conducting a class, a course of study, a lesson.

influencing a person (entering into, awakening, illuminating another person's mind and life).

providing resources and experiences, and explaining and interpreting them.

producing change and fostering development (in thoughts, feelings, character, and behavior).

stimulating and bringing out (evoking) inner disclosures (personal insights) and responses (actions of the learner's mind, soul, and body).

Obviously many of these ideas or "models" of education overlap, and something could be said for each of them. But we must do more than argue for any of them if we want to find the best answers to the question we have repeatedly raised: In what ways of teaching and learning are children, youth, or adults most likely to "get" the Word of Christ, the Christian Gospel, and thereby also the Spirit, power, and life of God?

To put the question in terms of the Spirit already implanted in the baptized and believing Christian: By what methods can we best serve to open the way for the Spirit of God to affect and direct the learner from within himself? No doubt the question could be worded also in terms of nurture and from many other viewpoints. All ideas of education have their characteristic methods, and we shall have to evaluate these methods in the light of our principles.

We might think we could easily settle and close the question of methods by quoting Eph. 6:4: "Bring them up in the discipline and instruction of the Lord." But we would still be faced with the necessity of establishing what the original Greek verse meant by the words *paideia* and *nouthesia*. They have been translated into a great variety of terms. We would also have to explain what we mean by such translations as "discipline and instruction" or "nurture and admonition." And the truth of the matter would depend on what we meant as well as on what the text said.

A MOST COMMON PATTERN

Since we cannot examine (in fact, may not even know) what often is meant by the various words and definitions for education, let us review briefly the most common methods that characterized formal education in our recent past and are to a large extent still dominant. How do most teachers teach, and what are the most common methods we ourselves use in the teaching of religion?

In a study of the teaching pattern of American high school teachers, Arno Bellack and his associates found that the two most common patterns of classroom teaching were teacher solicitation — student response, and teacher solicitation — student response — teacher reaction. The researchers concluded that the rules of the game are: (1) the teacher is to be the single most active person playing the game; and

(2) the pupil's primary task in the game is to respond to the teacher's solicitation.

In a similar study of teacher-learner interaction in elementary schools, Marie Hughes found that over 80 percent of the teachers were dominating in over half the acts they performed. Simple memory-recall was the most common activity solicited by the teachers. The extensive research findings of Prof. Ned Flanders and his associates were summarized by Flanders' rule of two-thirds: In the average classroom in America someone is talking two-thirds of the time; two-thirds of this is teacher-talk; and two-thirds of teacher-talk consists in efforts at direct influence (lecture, directions, or criticisms). The other third of the time the teacher is asking questions, reacting to students, or giving praise.[2]

All this simply goes to show that public schools still largely use teacher-dominated methods rather than creative learning procedures that depend on the workings of a spirit within the learner. This is still the case in spite of half a century of widespread educational writings and teacher training to the contrary! It is therefore quite likely and understandable that also in most church schools, and particularly in the teaching of religion, we would find a heavy reliance on one-way communication of words, facts, and abstract formulations through storytelling, lecturing, drilling, and other methods of *teacher presentations*.

Religion in schools and churches tends to be thought of as an organized subject (usually in a book — the Bible, the catechism, the lesson materials, etc.) instead of as a faith in a way of life and living. The chances are, therefore, that when learner response is solicited by the leader, questions and answers are given from the book or off the top of the head instead of from any depths of the heart. Learner activity is limited more or less to the recitation, workbook, and other testing methods that deal almost exclusively with factual knowledge and intellectual, abstract understanding.

Also the patterns of *adult* education in the church reflect in large measure the way adults were taught as children. "The average adult," said David Ernsberger, "expects his adult class to resemble the usually authoritarian class atmosphere he learned to know in grade school, high school, and even college. He expects to be told and regards himself mainly as a passive listener, *and this is especially true in the church.* . . . And the adults are going to continue to remain passive until the . . . adult leader takes steps to redefine his role in the group so as to alter the authoritarian role expectations which people hold in regard to his function."[3]

By now some readers may be fuming because they feel that what they are doing is being attacked and destroyed. But we are not denying the value of the traditional methods. Nor is this book recommending the use of activity and creative methods apart from or instead of in the service of the Word and Spirit of God. It is regrettable that activity methods came into disrepute through their misuse.

The rest of this chapter will try to show how traditional methods can be made more spiritual and therefore more interesting and effective. At the same time we have vital reasons for asking whether some of the newer methods are being used as much as they deserve to be. After all, why not change our methods if that's what we must do to improve our teaching and to increase the only kind of learning that has eternal value?

Ways of Involving the Learner

We discussed previously how human beings get involved in the Word or in any subject. Let us now apply these principles first to the traditional methods most of us use most often.

STORYTELLING AND TALKING

Lest anyone should think that our study has suggested the elimination of all presentations by the leader or teacher (or even by other members of a group), let us note that the relating of events recorded in the Bible (Biblical, salvation history) undoubtedly must continue to be one of the main methods of communicating the Christian faith. This necessity is in the very nature of the Christian religion. The Christian faith is a story that has its source and basis in history, the history recorded in the Sacred Scriptures.

Present-day emphasis on language that is alive and on "kerygmatic teaching" (the *proclaiming* of the Gospel) further underscores the need of telling not only "the old, old story of Jesus and His love" but *any* stories of this love of God. And they can be told by many kinds of methods and not just by the group leader. Visual material, dramatic methods, reading of books, presentations by students, group discussion of a story—all can serve to communicate the event. We ought not to restrict such storytelling to little children, for youth and adults also need to hear and recall "God's mighty deeds of old."

However, our study indicated that any recounting

of the great redemptive acts of God calls for something other than the telling of Bible stories simply as historical events. Without Gospel interpretation through personal witnessing (expressions of faith) by the storyteller, even the story of the birth of Jesus or of His death and resurrection can appear to be just a sentimental, tragic, or meaningless happening in the long ago and dead past, something students have heard before and are tired of hearing because it doesn't mean anything *to them*.

Someone has said: "Education is participation in meanings." At this point we need to recall what was said in Chapter 2 about ways of getting at "the inside story of an event" — the word of meaning beneath the surface of the happening. And we need to consider what was said about relating a story to the learner and his life, regardless of how the facts are communicated. The task of helping others see themselves in a story usually requires the use of *several* methods.

As the reported surveys indicated, the use of the question-answer method usually follows the telling of a story. Again, there is nothing wrong in asking questions to clarify a story, but a concern for spiritual values suggests that we make greater use of informal conversation and discussion. Formal questions too often require mere remembering of what was told or read. They seldom call for the personal thoughts, reactions, and decisions of the learner. Nor does the traditional question-answer method leave much room for deeper understandings that come when learners share personal experiences and personal insights.

What kind of questions are most likely to stimulate genuine participation in a discussion and not merely *forced* responses? Some indication was given in previous references to the art of leading discussions.[4] In this connection we might note again the importance of questions that confront the learner with an issue of life and with the necessity to think about the truth or meaning of a Word of God.

Important too for involving the learner in the Word of truth are all the other techniques of dialog, especially the communicator's eager listening and respectful responses to the questions and comments of the others in communication with him. This requires a quite different viewpoint and attitude than was expressed by the man who wrote, "Revelation cannot be discovered; it can only be proclaimed; that is, authoritatively proclaimed and listened to."[5]

If this is true, we must continue to prefer passive learners in our teaching of religion and can only make a superficial use of activity methods. But Jesus said, "Ask . . . seek . . . knock" in order to hear, see, and receive. And the Bereans were commended because they examined the Scriptures *to see* whether the things Paul and Silas said were true. (Acts 17:11)

INQUIRY AND DISCOVERY METHODS

This book has been saying that a person truly learns and knows something only as he actively participates in the learning experience as a person. Also the revelatory experiences of the Spirit of God must be felt and lived in order to be real. In a booklet called *Method* the author, a Lutheran parish pastor, wrote that after years of frustration and nightmarish dissatisfaction with traditional teaching methods, he came to the following conclusions:

A. Current methods are not beginning to exhaust the learning potential of our youth.

B. The core of a better method is this: That the

student himself investigate, discover, and express creatively the lessons to be learned.[6]

We noted the value of the inquiry method in connection with our previous discussions of personal insight or discernment. What are the steps in the inquiry process? The first need is an attitude of curiosity, interest, and wonder on the part of the investigator, the student.

But how can we stir up this interest? Some educators have recommended the so-called inductive approach (from concrete particulars to generalizations) in contrast to a deductive procedure (from a generalization to specific illustrations). But it doesn't really matter much where one begins when the concern is the discovery and understanding of a principle or truth of life.

To stimulate this interest, we have noted, someone must raise a question—a *real* question, a problem, an issue. This is why the inquiry or discovery method is also called the problem method. The teacher who raises really important problems of life does not ask little fact questions for their own sake. He inquires about facts only *in relation to the* big *question* under inquiry. There's a great difference between the two uses of facts. In the one the facts become important for their own sake; in the other they often are not important simply as isolated facts.

The problem and inquiry method of teaching challenges the learner to think, to be nosy, to risk being wrong with hunches or hypotheses until they are tested. The student who dares to express himself only when he is sure he knows the answers that others think are right is not likely to think, much less think for himself.

So the learner must feel free enough to be able

to be wrong in his search for truth and life. If he can't be wrong and forgiven in the church of Jesus Christ, I'm afraid His Spirit, the Spirit of God, is sadly absent. When absent, the Spirit cannot lead the learner into truth.

The inquiry method calls for a skillful use of questions that lead the student on in his own thinking and do not merely call for stock and "finished" answers. Inquiry uses questions for exploration and probing, for drilling *into* a lesson rather than for the drilling *of* a story or subject, for testing the spirits "to see whether they are of God," as the Bible recommends. (1 John 4:1)

When Socrates used questions, he not only *raised questions;* he *questioned* the students' *answers* so that they had to give the basis for their thinking and make a convincing case for what they said. This led to vital verbal interaction, or dialog.

David Suchman has illustrated another way in which questions can encourage genuine student inquiry. After presenting some material (content) — visually, as a rule — Suchman asks his students to try to discover *why* the happening, the phenomenon, the experiment occurred as it did. And he invites the students to ask *him* questions, to which he answers with counter-questions or simply yes and no, as in the Twenty Questions game.[7]

Children as well as adults are most inclined to think when they are given the opportunity to think about real problems and important questions. For pupils to become *students* (*seekers* after meanings, *users* of information, *discoverers* of truth, convinced *witnesses,* and actively involved *disciples*), we need to make the Christian faith and life a *quest,* as Thelen has called all true education. [8]

146

Back in 1905 William Bagley wrote: "The pupil is not to be told but led to see. . . . Whatever the pupil gains, whatever thought connections he works out, must be gained with the consciousness that he, the pupil, is the active agent—that he is, in a sense at least, the discoverer." [9] Even longer ago Herbert Spencer observed that "to give the net product of inquiry without the inquiry that leads to it is found to be both enervating and inefficient. General truths, to be of due and permanent use, must be earned." [10]

To develop the questioning mind and the skills that are needed for independent personal learning, we can use almost any kind of method. The value of any teaching technique is in the way it is used. For example, to give students the task of finding their own answers, we could make much greater use of directed reading, experimental projects, silent meditation, or thoughtful viewing of visuals and dramatic materials.

Such methods as these would give the Holy Spirit a chance to prompt some reflective thinking in the learner. We could also use, much more than we do, such research methods as interviewing of other people, studying of reference materials, and field trips for first-hand observation (of actual church life and church work, for example). By all means try some of these methods. You'll see how suddenly your students will get interested in religion.

Creative Learning Activities

Though most activity methods gain in purpose when used for inquiry, there is a still more deeply personal type of thinking that we might neglect if we did not become aware of the importance of the learner's own discoveries and his own responses.

I have already warned against expecting or, much worse, demanding *immediate* or *predetermined* responses of the Holy Spirit in the human spirit. But fruits of the Spirit can be expected when the Word of the Spirit is actually communicated. And we already noted the principle that such fruits are much more likely to flower and form when there is a climate of freedom in which the learner can branch out and grow by himself.

VALUES IN CREATIVE PROCEDURES

It's the age-old principle of "No impression without expression" but from a somewhat different point of view than in the past. Originally the principle emphasized the importance of some expression after impression, some "doing" to follow the learning or knowing of a subject or lesson. But the assumption was, more or less, that authoritative methods impress and creative methods are needed only for some expression that is mainly repetition, a coughing up or practicing of that which has been impressed.

On the other hand, those who went all out for expression often neglected the substance, the Word, that must be taught and learned. They often tolerated pointless, meaningless, worthless activities.

Today psychologists and philosophers of education do not make a sharp distinction between the two concerns. Our principles of personal participation in learning to know the Christ also suggest that impressions and insights are gained *through* thinking and expression. We recognize that responses, activity experiences, and expressions can *lead to* impressions and understandings as well as *flow from* them.

Because this is true, the great battle that has been going on in the church over methods of religious education can come to a halt. So-called creative methods truly can be teaching and learning activities and not just entertainment or "something extra" to make religious education interesting or a little more palatable if there is time. What then, besides dialog, are some techniques that give the learner opportunities to express himself creatively as a person?

INDIVIDUALIZING OUR TEACHING

Many of the more creative methods could be classified as *individual* procedures rather than group methods. There is no doubt that for creative and personal expression and experiences, the members as well as the leader of any kind of group must have occasions for uniquely individual communications. Also the reverse is true, that without opportunity for uniquely individual expressions, human beings will not be as creative as they could be.

I have already mentioned the kind of settings, relationships, and climate that are needed if the uniquely individual spirit of the learner is to blossom and flourish. Our focus now is on the *methods*, in or out of the classroom, that encourage creative learning and expression. What are ways of encouraging individuals to reveal themselves — their thoughts and feelings, their faith and hopes, their lives? And what are some channels for individual expression that serve to make Christian communication more spiritual and creative?

Techniques for getting the individual student to raise his own questions and to study for personal discoveries have been noted. A further possibility is the *recording and sharing of findings*. This writing and presentation by the student can be an essay, a book review, or simply a short report. Many other types of writing serve to encourage the writer to think and discover personal meaning of God's truth: letters, a short story, a poem, a hymn, a diary, an editorial, a play, a short biography or autobiography — any kind of writing by which the *student* would be expressing, recording, and communicating.

Those who find it easier to express themselves by means of visual languages rather than verbal need the revealing and inspiring experiences that the creation of pictures and other forms of visual images and art can provide. The value of the arts as media for learning will be discussed at length in the next section, so here we shall limit ourselves to a listing of types of visuals or visual-art activity. Through any of these the individual learner might express his understandings, feelings, and faith either by creating the visuals or by interpreting them or by both.

Even though groupings and labels always overlap, the following classification might do for a start: drawing, painting, photography, sculpture; the making of murals, posters, films, cartoons, maps, charts, scrapbooks, objects; or the use of any of these. In addition there are the many types of construction activities provided by handcraft or building projects — the designing and construction of a model church building, for example. The preparation of exhibits could include all types of creative activities and their created materials.

Visual languages can, of course, become dead forms and false communication just as readily as verbal messages can. Usually visuals need to be combined with words for clarity, understanding, and effect. Even the great mime Marcel Marceau

150

can't do without the mouthing of words and the use of words on posters. But by their very nature visuals seem particularly suited to the communicating of a *spirit* and thereby the *messages* of a spirit.

GROUP ACTIVITIES AND EXPERIENCES

Some of the creative activities mentioned under individual methods lend themselves also to group use, but great paintings are seldom the product of a committee process. On the other hand, drama, which combines the use of movement and oral speech with visual forms, usually involves more than one person.

Also in group activities the individual must mesh with the subject matter in a personal response with feeling if the experience is to be a spiritual activity. In the discussion of art media (next chapter) more will be said about the need of emotional involvement on the part of the hearer or viewer as well as the communicator. For now, let us note some of the many types of dramatic activities that lend themselves as methods of expressing the Christian faith.

Drama can be the visual acting out of a message in many forms other than formal plays: role-playing (including psychodrama or sociodrama, in which individuals try out the role of persons in real-life emotional or social problems); the use of puppets, marionettes, and dolls; chancel dramas; pageants; tableaux; pantomime; informal acting out of stories (with interpretations); creative play; etc.

But does drama really deserve a much greater place than it has in most church parishes? The answer depends on whether the drama serves to communicate a truth of God or whether it at least stimulates a thoughtful study of the Word of Christ and of His

151

Spirit. Are dramatic methods *practical* enough for most study groups or classes? How could they be used in a typical Sunday church school, for example? These questions can be answered only in the attempted use of dramatics. As soon as anyone really wants to use them, he finds them practical.

So why use drama as a means and method of communicating and nurturing the Christian faith? Dramatic methods can be very disturbing in more ways than one. Once when there was a great agitation over a play scheduled for a Sunday school convention, some people even said that nothing as serious as the Word of God ought to be presented dramatically. (I can remember the time when people were offended by the use of films and filmstrips in the church.) Others maintained that if the dramatic method is used, it should present only the recorded Biblical facts, preferably the very words of the text.

But our principles of spiritual communication have maintained that something *more* is needed than a re-presentation or reproduction of facts and events as recorded. Dramatic writing and acting are particularly suited to this task of *interpreting* the Bible and the Christian faith both historically and in contemporary and personal terms.

Because the purpose of artful drama is to illuminate eternal truths and to involve both the communicator and the receiver in the underlying meanings of a situation or event, the use of dramatic methods can be of great service to God and His church. So in order to communicate His Word with greater power and effect, perhaps we ought to use dramatic methods much more often than we do.

The use of *music* for communion with God and the *creation* of music as an expression of His Spirit also deserve far more consideration than this brief mention of it indicates. Though this medium and method of communication may at first seem foreign and remote to the ordinary task of a Christian parent or church school leader, music can speak to the heart and inspire the human spirit as nothing else can.

Music lends itself readily to creative participation especially in the production of it. Children, youth, or adults who sing in a choir or who simply experience the singing of Christian hymns, carols, canticles, and folk songs hear and learn the Word of God in spirit. Thereby they are strengthened in their Christian faith.

Related to the issue of the unit (the need of activities and creative methods for the learning of the Word and Spirit of God) is the question of learning by experience. For years there was a violent debate over John Dewey's contention that all vital learning is through experience. There were good reasons for much of the concern over the ways in which so-called progressive education used Dewey's theory. But now experience and doing are generally acknowledged as essential to learning. Also religious education programs call for the use of experience and activity methods.

On the basis of our primary principle we can be certain of this: *Without the experience of God's Spirit no Christian learning occurs,* no matter what one thinks of John Dewey and progressive education. Much of the argument over experience methods and the weaknesses in their use may be caused by a limited concept of the word "experience." In any case, real-life human behavior (both individual and social, past as well as present and future) can serve to relate the truth of the Word of God to human experience.

Haven't we all said, "Experience is the best teacher," even though this isn't always true? There are various kinds of experience. All of them—direct, indirect, or imagined—can serve to illuminate the eternal truths of God. Thereby they lead the learner to communion with God and the experience of His Spirit.[11]

8

Therefore,
if any one is in Christ,
he is a new creation;
the old has passed away,
behold, the new has come.

St. Paul

2 Corinthians 5:17

8

MEDIA OF REVELATION AND FAITH

This book has been saying that to receive, to learn, and to know a communication is to respond as a person. And to respond is to be spiritually involved and changed.

But for learner involvement in the Christian faith and for God-produced changes within people and their societies, the Word of faith (the Scriptures, the Gospel, and the person Jesus Christ) must somehow become related to the learner's personal life and world. The previous chapter therefore suggested that we give the learner opportunities to experience the Word of truth and life through activities of thinking, expressing, personal witnessing, and actions —in short, through personal participation.

This participation, when God-induced and spiritual, is never perfunctory or forced—never matter-of-fact, half-hearted, surface participation, as far too many activities in the church are. The person moved by the Spirit, even if not *filled* with the Spirit, acts out of the creative promptings of his *own* spirit.

In considering the methods that require and lead to the personal participation of the learner, we briefly gave some attention to creative activity and especially individual creative activity. In a sense every method a teacher uses calls for learning activity, and all activities in the church are intended to nurture the new life of the Spirit of Christ within the learner. From this point of view also the lecture and story-telling methods can be truly creative. But on the other hand, not every activity is a creative activity.

We noted certain practical principles and methods that make for more creative teaching and learning. A stimulating leader or teacher asks genuine questions that require thinking. He prefers *personal* thinking and work and provides opportunities for *individual* learning and creative expression. The person who follows these practices will find, as a rule, more life and learning in his group than the person who mainly reads or tells, no matter how spirited the latter's intentions or manner might be.

Now very much related to the foregoing is another question: What are the *forms* by which the Word of God is most powerfully communicated? It isn't enough to answer that the means of experiencing God's grace and Spirit is the Word. We have acknowledged the role of the Word in the very first section. Here we want to know what the best means or media are for *communicating* the Word. To put the question in another way: By what media of the Word is the *Spirit* of the Word most likely to be experienced deeply?

Messages, methods, and media influence and often determine one another. In this section we shall focus on certain neglected but powerful *media.* Whether we consider these media to be *methods* of communication or prefer to think of them as forms of the *message,* we shall see that media inherently involve particular kinds of *methods* even as methods involve certain kinds of *materials.*

The Arts as Media of Word and Spirit

A number of people who have thought and written about education in recent years have concluded that what this world needs in order to make it more human if not divine is education through art.[1] Why? The answer may become evident as we consider art as a product of the human spirit. Thereupon let us ask how the arts might serve to educate both the church and the world "in the Spirit."

VESSELS OF TRUTH AND VOICES OF SPIRIT

The reader might first ask himself, "What do I usually mean by the word 'art'?" On hearing the word, most people probably think of drawings and paintings. But the word also carries much broader meanings. It can refer to the whole field of knowledge and activity that at times is called "the arts." It can include or be modified by such terms as "visual art," "dramatics," "the literary arts," "musical art," etc. This chapter will be talking about art (the arts) in general.

There are many different views of what deserves to be called art in any of its fields. We need not (fortunately) try to settle the debate that has gone on for ages, though it's always interesting (and usually quite revealing) to find out what others think is good art. In discussing the arts as *communication* Robert Wunderlich wrote: "A true artist is never content to deal merely with the surface of his subject. He tries to get beneath the surface, to lay bare some underlying and often-overlooked truth." Later, in considering the effects of art as *response*, ·Professor Wunderlich continued: "All great art encompasses still another dimension in human life. It reaches us at the deepest level of our awareness, at a level 'too deep for tears,' as one writer has characterized a Beethoven symphony." [2]

If we concluded from the quotation that the two mentioned functions of art (communication and response) can ever be separated, we would be drawing a *false* distinction. A response is an effect of a communication, and a communication communicates its effect. By his distinction between communication and response Wunderlich is merely calling attention to the two-fold but nevertheless one-and-the-same role that art can play. By communicating a word (an insight, a revelation, a message) possessed by a human spirit (the communicator or artist), art *thereby* communicates a spirit that affects the spirit of other human beings.

In an article about drama I once wrote: "One cannot expect to deal adequately with this question [of what is art] in a paragraph or two. However, there is a rather commonly expressed criterion: Any kind of communication does not deserve to be called art unless it presents a meaning—a view or principle of life, so to speak—in an illuminating and striking way." [3]

This oversimplified definition of art underscores the principle that *to be art*, a painting, piece of writing, or dramatic presentation must do more than re-present nature, facts, or even thoughts. A bare, cold, strictly objective presentation that lacks interpretation, imaginative treatment, and the personal involvement of the communicator is not art, though it may be *called* music or poetry or drama or a painting or a story. It is sterile repetition—copying, mouthing, parroting, lifeless imitating.

True, the artist perceives, discovers, and reveals by his art the truths and values that already exist.

It is only in this sense that he creates. But he creates through *personal discovery and unique expression.*

Art is creative also in a second sense. As Professor Wunderlich indicated, art not only mediates a truth of life as the artist perceives it and thereby is a vessel and communicator of a word or message; but in communicating its message in the forms of a visualized, dramatized, or musically moving *spirit,* art also serves to create insights and a given spirit *in others.* Thereby art educates and changes people in the inner depths of their spirit.

This is the kind of education that makes a lasting difference and therefore really matters and counts. It is a quite different kind of education than the learning and knowing of words and facts apart from meanings or the doing of what one has been told or trained to do. It is the possession of a subject as a *discipline of life,* as a faith in the very heart of a person's being.

The serious artist of the 20th century is not concerned with the imitation of nature, the expression of beauty, or the mere presentation of an ideal or feeling. Techniques and considerations of medium, color, light, lines, movement, balance, harmony, and the like are all incidental to a concern for *truths of life.* Also in the literary arts, forms and substances and techniques are used to express a significant, thought-provoking question or meaning.

In discussing education through visual art in particular, Herbert Read said: "Art is literally . . . spirit informing matter." [4] This readiness of all the arts to serve as a vehicle of truth and a voice of a spirit is what makes the products of artistic activity so very suited to the education of the human spirit. In their very nature the arts lend themselves as most appropriate media also for the Word and Spirit of God.

Many related spiritual values and therefore advantages in the educational use of the arts could be mentioned. In speaking indirectly through symbols (figures, characters, pictures, actions) art challenges a person to think, and stimulates and deepens personal insights. By using the kinds of symbolic language that we previously noted are characteristic of spiritually religious language, art allows the freedom of the mind and spirit of both the creator and the consumer, the communicator and the learner. This is the kind of freedom needed if the Word and Spirit of God are to speak to both of the human parties in communication.

Many Christians want everything in their religion spelled out plainly, defined, codified, and repeated *ad nauseam* "to the last letter." But "the letter" kills; it is the Spirit that gives life. To permit the Spirit of God to speak to His disciples, Jesus taught through word pictures and actions and object lessons and illustrative stories. He placed a child in the midst of His disciples for a lesson in faith. He pointed to birds for a lesson in trust. He often referred to history for His revelations of present and eternal truths of God.

Matthew wrote: "Indeed He [Jesus] said nothing to them without a parable." This was to fulfill what was spoken by a prophet of God who had written: "I will open my mouth in parables. I will utter what has been *hidden* since the foundation of the world" (Matt. 13:34-35). When the disciples asked Jesus why He spoke in parables, He answered: "Because seeing

162

they do not see, and hearing they do not hear, nor do they understand" (v. 13). And Mark and Luke report Jesus as saying: "*So that* they may indeed see but not perceive, and may indeed hear but not understand." (Mark 4:12; Luke 8:10)

Jesus spoke in parables and picture language to prevent an easy, surface understanding and acceptance of His teachings without a change of heart. He did not teach in plain and simple language that no one could misunderstand. Why not? Because God's Word is *more than words.* It is truth and meaning and spirit and life. These can be destroyed by plain, dull, belabored talk that leaves little to the Spirit of God in the Word and in the learner.

ART IN THE TEACHING OF RELIGION

What I have been trying to say about art in general applies equally to art that serves to communicate God. We need not try to distinguish between art and religious art and Christian art. In fact it may be dangerous to do so. Such distinctions could lead us to think that an artistic activity or product is religious or Christian or art simply because it appears in a church building, a Christian school, or a religious program, or because it presents a religious subject or was produced by Christians.

Such conclusions obviously could be completely false. The question depends entirely on whether the particular art activity or product communicates a Word from God. As Walter Nathan has said, "Christian truth does not reside in externals but in the artist's work."[5] Even though we can say that the truth of God does reside in externals or forms of the Word when the Spirit is embodied in the forms, we have all seen pictures and plays or have read stories

163

of religious subjects that were neither art nor religious nor Christian in spirit.

At the same time we Christians need to appreciate (much more than most of us do) that the arts can be most suitable media for the carrying out of the church's mission and educational ministry. Martin Luther praised music as the handmaiden of theology and desired to put all the arts to the service of God.[6] Even the very young and the illiterate can "read" pictures and "sense" truth and feel the spirit of music and drama.

The arts, we said, allow personal reflection and meditation. Thereby they permit the Spirit of God to do what no Christian communicator may dare to do without getting in the way of the Spirit. Whenever we humans try to enter *directly* into the inner life of other people (by forcing our way into their thoughts and feelings or by imposing our thoughts and will upon them), we are likely to bruise or drive away or destroy their spirit. Regardless of how much we want to influence others, we must remember that our very desire may get in the way of our desired outcome unless we actually trust in God for our desired effects.

By presenting a Word of God in symbolic form, art stimulates and permits the mind of the receiver to relate the Word to his own human experiences, understandings, and life. By speaking in symbols, art makes the Word of life actually a word of *Life*—for the present and for the present person, even when it speaks of the past. It relates and interprets eternal truths to the world of time and change and action.

To illustrate: As a religion teacher I might present an early medieval picture of a feathered man with wings (an archangel) holding a balance scale with a naked human being crouched on one of the plates

164

and begging for help. Imagine on the other side of the picture a great sea monster spewing forth some gruesome-looking goblins (little devils) who plunk themselves gleefully on the scale and unbalance it.

If instead of lecturing about this 13th-century picture, I would allow the *picture* to speak to my students, I would find that they would be quite ready to think about my questions. They might also discover *by themselves* the medieval idea of angels and devils, some false theology concerning God's way of judging a person, and most important of all, the Gospel of the Christian's hope for life and salvation in Christ. In like manner I could use poetry or a story or a song (read or told or dramatized or sung—it doesn't matter).

In wanting others to reflect personally on the Word of the Spirit and thereby to be led into all truth by the *Spirit*, we preachers and teachers of religion have the best of reasons to use the arts—for communication or for creative expression. Of course also works of art deliver their message only when the persons addressed receive and open up and accept and use the message. This is why the experiencing of a work of art and learning through art also require *communion* with it, not just a one-way communication.

Holy Communication Through Worship and the Sacraments

The use of the arts in Christian religious education can be a lifetime study. So we turn lastly to another much-neglected though distinctly suited medium of Word and Spirit, namely worship. From a Christian viewpoint, the creation and thoughtful appreciation of art can be worship. Furthermore, formal worship incorporates many types of art and in a sense is an art. Thus what was said about art applies also to worship. But worship has some additional advantages as an educational medium.

First we need to define the word "worship." This term has almost as many meanings as the word "art." The first meaning the word brings to mind is probably the act of prayer (private or corporate) and hymn singing. But a person can say prayers and sing hymns without really worshiping. The *spirit* of the action determines whether singing and praying are truly worship. And a spirit of worship can be in any kind of human action.

Christian worship is the response of the human spirit to the God revealed in Jesus Christ. It is the response of Christian faith, which in its fullest sense is a way of looking at life and a way of living—an offering of ourselves to Him who died for us but rose again and now reigns eternally as Lord and Savior of the world.

But in a formal sense the word "worship" refers to the liturgical life, the *leitourgia* (Greek) or, literally, people's works of service (that is, services of worship). These find their forms and expression in all the arrangements for private and public acts of worship and particularly in the orders for *corporate* services of worship.

In a narrower sense "the liturgy" simply refers to the "order of service" or certain forms for community worship. Even more specifically it refers to the service in which the Lord's Supper is celebrated. However, such a narrow limitation in the use of the word "liturgy" robs us of its more enriching refer-

166

ences. I shall therefore be using the word as synonymous with worship.

So next we shall be considering briefly "the liturgy" and the liturgical life, meaning all the arrangements and procedures, both actual and possible, that may serve as aids to worship. In thinking of worship as direct communication and communion with God, we may hope to find in the forms and in the doing of the liturgy what could be, if it isn't, the church's most promising source of God's power.

Perhaps we can also find out why so-called "high church" attention to the liturgical life often becomes known for its evident *failure* to give people, particularly children, the experience of communion with God and a faith and life rich in the fruits of God's Spirit. Anyone who has seen the state of the highly liturgical churches of England or Sweden has serious reasons to question the spiritual value and power of liturgical forms. This fact too must be faced in considering liturgical revival to be the greatest hope of life in the church, as some people do.

THE LITURGICAL LIFE

What can the liturgy or liturgical life mean, and how might it serve to communicate the Word and Spirit of God? Would most Protestant as well as Roman Catholic churches profit greatly from a liturgical renewal? Could a wider and deeper participation in the liturgy by children as well as adults contribute vitally to their education in the Christian faith?

In whatever way it is understood, the liturgy serves to communicate the Word of God. It does so first of all in the arrangement of the church year. By its observance Christians hear of Christ and meet Him in the great festivals that are celebrated annually.

167

A minimum church year observance would include Advent, Christmas, Epiphany, Lent, Easter, Ascension Day, and Pentecost. The weekly observance of a Lord's Day on the first day of the week, the day of Christ's resurrection, also was designed to be a reminder of His living, victorious presence, and annually presents the whole circle of His instructions to His followers in every age.

Especially the gathering of God's people on the Lord's Day for "breaking of bread and prayer" (Holy Communion and worship) is a present witness of faith in the living Christ and His sacrificial, redemptive love. It is also a means of hearing regularly the Gospel of salvation—through the words of absolution, the Scripture readings, the sermon, and the great Biblical songs of prayer and praise in the liturgical service—and children as well as adults are blessed by such regular communion with God.

As Christians gather together for worship and the "breaking of bread," the risen, living Christ who gave Himself into death for the life of the world is in the midst of the assembly, for He said: "Where two or three are gathered in My name, there am I in the midst of them" (Matt. 18:20). He is present not only in the Word and Sacrament but also by His Spirit in His people—in their silent meditations on Him or His Word and in their expressions of worship. This is why the worship life of the church is very important to the education of its members.

God's Word of life is proclaimed also through the liturgical actions or ritual (as when the pastor makes the sign of the cross or holds up his hands in blessing). The Christian faith is communicated, too, through signs and symbols in stained-glass windows, paintings, sculpture, candles, and other objects; through the architecture of the place for worship; by the music and hymns and choir anthems; and through the demeanor and actions both of the people and of the officiants engaged in worship.

Throughout the history of the Christian church the sacraments of Holy Baptism and the Lord's Supper have had special importance in the life of Christian faith and worship. The baptismal font customarily is placed at the entrance or in the front of the nave of the house of worship—or at least in an annex—to symbolize that this rite of initiation into the kingdom and mysteries of Christ is an entrance into the life of His church. The Lord's Supper (also called the Holy Eucharist, meaning Feast of Thanksgiving) was celebrated daily by the earliest Christians, and this "breaking of bread" has continued to be a regular part of Christian worship.

Some Christians call the blessed supper that Christ instituted "Holy Communion." So is any other kind of communication or communion with God. Also the sacrament of Baptism is a medium by which one receives the Spirit and grace of God and enters into a holy communion with Him. But the celebration of these sacraments and a conscious living in their meaning have a particularly great value. How so?

THE POWER OF THE SACRAMENTS

The two sacraments established by Jesus for the growth and strength of His church are liturgical actions that uniquely present and communicate the gift of divine forgiveness and life available through faith in Him. St. Augustine called these sacraments "the visible Word." By means of visible signs and symbolic acts as well as words, the Gospel of Christ's redemptive death and the promise of

169

a new and everlasting life through faith in Him is proclaimed.

In short, the sacraments present the summed-up Word of the Scriptures, the same Word that is taught by any faithful Christian witness. They are another form of the Word, by which Jesus Christ unites Himself with the members of His body.

Wherein, then, does the *special* power of the sacraments and their use lie? Or perhaps we should fearlessly ask: *Do* the sacraments have the special powers that Christians believe they have? How could the German poet Heinrich Heine insist toward the end of his life that, though he had been baptized, he had never been converted? Why is it that literally millions of baptized people give little if any evidence of having Christian faith? How can it be that even we who participate in the liturgical life of the church and regularly receive the Lord's Supper often seem far from strong in spirit or "filled with the Spirit"?

If all the people in our community were baptized and all the members of our parish (the children and youth too) went to church every Sunday and all (including the children) celebrated the Lord's Supper every Sunday, would they become more Christian? Would they be more alive as members of Christ's body? Is the person who always attends church and frequently participates in Holy Communion more spiritual, more in communion with God, a better image of God in his life, than the people who don't?

Not necessarily! To avoid the folly of formalism we must admit this. We have already acknowledged *negative* evidence in "high" as well as "low" churches. The sacraments and the rites and rituals that have been built around them present the very heart of Christ's redemptive action, but as our previous principles emphasized, words and therefore also words and actions used in liturgical worship can lose their meaning. The "practice" of the liturgy and the celebration of the sacraments can become perfunctory, empty tradition.

Such formalism, which constantly threatens the very life of any religion that has its roots in the past, can become a work of righteousness for the officiants and the participants. And such formalism is a revulsion to God. We dare not forget this in considering the urgent need of more attention to worship and the sacraments in teaching the Christian religion.

Wherein, then, lies our hope? As with everything else, our hope lies in God, who is the Spirit. He is the eternal Word revealed most vividly in the life, death, resurrection, and ascension of Christ into the glories of heaven. In this kingdom of heaven the Lord of life reigns victoriously at the right hand of God *through His Spirit*, whom He poured upon His first disciples and continues to give to His disciples in all ages. And God's kingdom continues to come through Christ's reign until finally "the kingdom of the world has become the kingdom of our Lord and of His Christ." (Rev. 11:15)

But again we must note that God sends His Spirit of power in Christ through His Word, the Word of God's grace and forgiveness, the Gospel of His gracious love in Jesus Christ. And this Word, this Gospel of the kingdom of God, must be *communicated;* it must be taught effectively—*by God*—by the experience of His Spirit in the Word.

This truth or principle applies also to the sacraments. They present the Word, which is the sword of God's Spirit (Eph. 6:17), and we can be certain that this sword is potent (the power of God). But to *actually* communicate the Word by which the Spirit of Christ is received and experienced, the liturgy and the sacraments must be presented as the presence and work of Jesus Christ in the *present* and for the persons involved.

In other words, the liturgy and the sacraments must be heard and seen as the gracious Word of God's forgiving love given personally to the participant. This may require more careful and frequent explanation of the meaning of the liturgy and the sacraments than we normally give — to youth and adults as well as to children.

Furthermore, by the *Word* in the liturgy and in the sacraments the participant must be challenged to a *response* of the mind, heart, and life. Nothing will happen to a person by a thoughtless participation in a worship service or by "receiving" the sacraments without a *celebrating* of their meaning. People who do not participate in the liturgy or who daydream during a sermon or who don't respond to the sacraments in faith and love are not blessed by them. We can be sure of this.

TEACHING THE SACRAMENTS AND WORSHIP

What, then, must we do to become transmitters and "transformers" of the power of God in the liturgy and the sacraments so that others might receive the Spirit of God also through these means? This much we must acknowledge before there will be a great revival of spiritual life through liturgical, sacramental worship: More attention will have to be given to the Gospel meanings of these forms, and this requires *education* — education for liturgical worship — in all the schools of the church.

More thought needs to be given to the meaningful

teaching of Christian worship that finds its heart in a festive celebration of the church year, a weekly participation in the Lord's Supper or at least in a public service, and the living out of the life that one enters and receives via Holy Baptism. The Roman Catholic Church, which presently is undergoing a distinct liturgical renewal, is giving some attention to the subject.[7] But all churches that believe in liturgical forms and place high value on the sacraments risk the danger of using these forms without the power of the Word unless they teach the *meaning* of these forms.

And we must give more thought and attention also to the sacraments. If a Christian's baptism is to be a continuing source of spiritual refreshment, it will have to be more than a one-time social event that usually takes place in one's infancy. Christians must learn to "see" the symbolic meanings of their baptism and the rituals of the baptismal service. This requires the study of the sacrament and especially its Word of promises. The meanings of this Word are the power that first bury the baptized person into a death with Christ and then raise him with the risen and living Christ to life in His church and kingdom. (Rom. 6:3-8)

For example, one can think of baptism as a washing away of sins, as an entering into the ark of Christ's church, or as a crossing through water from slavery to freedom (like the exodus of the children of Israel). It is through such symbolic thinking that the promises and actions of God become evident and effectual. Such thinking must be learned.

Likewise participation in the Lord's Supper truly becomes the experience of a "power beyond words" when it is actually a remembering of the sacrificial,

173

atoning death of Christ and a "holy communion" of the participants with their everliving Lord. Children, too, can learn to know the Eucharist as Christ's continuing gift of Himself — the Bread and Wine of Life — received through the physical bread and wine of His Holy Supper. But again, this kind of learning requires more reference to this sacrament than Protestant children ordinarily experience.

What I have barely indicated in regard to the sacraments also needs to be said in reference to the whole liturgical life that the church has built around the central events of Christ's life and their Gospel meaning. The church year and liturgical worship forms communicate Christian doctrine, but in the form of celebrations. When the observance of these occasions and participation in them are understood and become the personal expression of the individual participant, then the *Spirit* of the Word is heard and felt. Then too, an inspiring, transforming communion with God occurs.

But such experiences in worship require also a teaching and learning of the forms. It may even demand the use of *new* forms that will carry the living Spirit of God and the life in Christ to the world of today, particularly to its children and youth. "New wine must be put into fresh wineskins," said Jesus. (Luke 5:38)

Some Necessary Conclusions

In reflecting back on some of the main points of our study, we may need to ask:

— What kind of Christian faith do we want people to have?

—What kind of experiences will serve to give them a personal, inner, transforming faith?

—How must our local churches and church schools change in order to provide a better ministry of the Word as a Word of *life*, the Word of the *Spirit*, of *God?*

—What necessary conclusions about our teaching of religion must we draw in honest and dead-serious dedication to the ministry of Christ and of His Gospel?

To benefit as much as possible from the book, the reader was urged to do his own thinking on the issues that were considered. Now he is asked to thoughtfully determine his own conclusions and actions. Only by such a process will improvements in Christian communication and education actually take place.

In our world of rapid and great changes, such improvements in communication are crucial to the whole life and mission of the church. At the same time we can be certain that the Spirit of God gives Christians with good and honest hearts the grace and power to serve Him creatively and victoriously in any time and place. "Behold, I am coming soon," said Jesus in the Revelation of St. John, "bringing My recompense, to repay everyone for what he has done. . . . The Spirit and the Bride say, 'Come.' And let him who hears say, 'Come.'" (Rev. 22:12, 17)

NOTES

1. HOW GOD STILL SPEAKS

1. A book by John Harrell titled *Teaching Is Communicating* (New York: The Seabury Press, 1965) shows the relation of theology to a psychological theory of communication and applies both to the use of visual materials in religious education. Other references for further reading will follow.
2. The study is reported in *Child Concepts of God*, by Oliver Graebner (River Forest, Ill.: Lutheran Education Association, 1960).
3. This is the question being asked by many recent books in theology, such as *Catechesis of Revelation*, by Gabriel Moran (New York: Herder and Herder, 1966).

2. KNOWING PERSONALLY AND BELIEVING IN

1. The theologian who wants to go into this subject more deeply might read *Truth and the Person in Christian Theology*, by Hugh Vernon White (New York: Oxford University Press, 1963).
2. What it means to be a person and to know a person is brilliantly described by the famous Christian psychiatrist Paul Tournier in *The Meaning of Persons* (New York: Harper, 1957).
3. For example, a Roman Catholic writer, while acknowledging Christ and the Bible as the Word of God, might tend to refer to the traditions and witness of the church as the living Word. The existentialist theologian, on the other hand, would probably be referring to a subjective experience.
4. Gabriel Moran, *God Still Speaks* (London: Burns & Oates, 1967), p. 83.

3. GETTING TO KNOW GOD

1. Michael Polanyi, *Personal Knowledge* (Chicago: The University of Chicago Press, 1958).
2. A number of experimental studies have shown that the reception of identical messages varies widely from ordinary interpretations when they are attributed to influential persons or are presented by well-liked and trusted people. See *The People's Choice*, by P. F. Lazarsfeld, B. Berlson, and H. Gaudet (New York: Columbia University Press, 1948).
3. Herbert T. Mayer, *Interpreting the Holy Scriptures* (St. Louis: Concordia Publishing House, 1967).
4. James Barr, in *The Semantics of Biblical Language* (London: Oxford University Press, 1961), has convincingly demonstrated this point.
5. Donald D. Evans, *The Logic of Self-Involvement* (London: SCM Press Ltd., 1963).

6. Martin H. Franzmann, "What Is Truth?" *Interaction*, IV, 1 (October 1963), 21.
7. J. Piaget and Ronald Goldman in particular have established this principle through extensive research.

4. THE LANGUAGE GOD SPEAKS

1. As important as the reading of articles and books on love is a personal thinking about the subject. Among the helpful books from a Christian viewpoint are Reuel Howe, *Herein Is Love* (New York: The Seabury Press, 1956); and Paul E. Johnson, *Christian Love* (New York: Abingdon-Cokesbury Press, 1951).
2. Daniel A. Prescott, *Role of Love in Human Development* (Austin, Tex.: A Hogg Foundation Reprint, 1959). Originally published in *Journal of Home Economics*, March 1952.
3. Ibid., p. 4.
4. For an elaboration of this thesis, see *The Silent Language* by Edwin T. Hall (New York: Doubleday & Co., 1959. [Paperback, Greenwich, Conn.: Fawcett Publications, Inc., 1961]).
5. Reuel Howe's *The Miracle of Dialogue* (New York: The Seabury Press, 1963) is required reading for a more thorough study of dialog.
6. Ibid., p. 37.

5. SPEAKING FOR GOD

1. This material appeared substantially as it is in *Interaction*, IV, 10 (July 1964), 12—14, and is used by permission of the publisher.
2. Such a conclusion was the mistake of the child-centered movement in religious education and could easily become the folly of a current emphasis on the experience of God through the secular world.
3. Gabriel Moran, *God Still Speaks* (London: Burns & Oates, 1967).
4. Arnold Ingen-Housz, "Bearing Witness, Fundamental Task of the Teacher of Religion," in *Faith and Commitment*, ed. Mark J. Link (Chicago: Loyola University Press, 1964), p. 91.
5. Helmut Thielicke, *The Trouble with the Church* (New York: Harper & Row, 1965), p. 5.
6. The three theses first appeared in the *Harvard Business Review* (July 1952) in an article titled "Barriers and Gateways to Communication." They were subsequently incorporated into other articles.
7. F. H. Drinkwater, "The Use of Words: A Problem of Both Content and Method," in *Shaping the Christian Message*, ed. Gerard S. Sloyan (Glen Rock, N. J.: Paulist Press, 1963), p. 196.
8. Ibid., pp. 193—210.
9. Ian T. Ramsey, *Religious Language* (New York: The Macmillan Co., paperback edition, 1963).

6. LEARNING THROUGH THE SPIRIT

1. Most of the principles are among the 50 propositions presented by Goodwin Watson in the booklet titled *What Psychology Can We Trust?* (New York: Bureau of Publications, Teachers College, Columbia University, 1961).